HOW TO PLAY BETTER CHESS

Also by Fred Reinfeld:

HOW TO BE A WINNER AT CHESS

HOW TO PLAY CHESS LIKE A CHAMPION

HOW TO GET MORE OUT OF CHESS

CHESS IN A NUTSHELL

A NEW APPROACH TO CHESS MASTERY

THE COMPLETE CHESS COURSE

THE GREAT CHESS MASTERS AND THEIR GAMES

THE COMPLETE BOOK OF CHESS TACTICS

WINNING CHESS OPENINGS

THE CHESS MASTERS ON WINNING CHESS

HOW TO BE A WINNER AT CHECKERS

HOW TO PLAY BETTER CHESS

by Fred Reinfeld

HANOVER HOUSE

Garden City, New York

1961

Library of Congress Catalog Card Number 61-9898

INTRODUCTION

In all times and climes, writers on chess have united in enthusiastic praise of the delightful complexities of the game. No one knows who first called chess "the royal game," but it is a term that has deservedly endured for centuries.

Yet the very attractiveness of chess creates a drawback. For this attractiveness springs from the manifold possibilities that are inherent in the game. After only a few moves, "anything can happen." So far, so good. But how does the aspiring student master this welter of possibilities? There's the rub. And how does one boil down all these complexities in a book of average size and length?

Common sense calls for one solution: the reader must be told what is most needful for him to know. If he gets the larger picture, the grand outlines, the basic points, then the game will fall into a manageable perspective. No matter how complex the game may become, such a player will feel at home in the complications because he is guided by basic principles. And there is an important psychological nuance here: such knowledge is not only helpful—it is comforting. For that knowledge breeds assurance.

What then are the indispensable features of the opening, middle game, and endgame?

In the opening, there is one factor which outweighs everything else—the importance of the center. The struggle for control of the center motivates all opening play, and the knowledge and skill with which this struggle is conducted make all the difference. Whether a player has good or bad prospects in the middle game will depend on how he played the opening.

When we turn to the middle game, we find that we must consider several facets: there are problems of *strategy*; of *tactics*; and of *defense*. Actually all these problems are interrelated. But in our discussion it is useful to separate them, so that they can be studied more easily. There is a widespread impression that the middle game—the most fascinating aspect of chess—yields up its secrets only to heaven-storming geniuses. But anyone who reads this section attentively will soon see that any average player, given the right material, can improve his game systematically.

The same thought applies to the endgame. Most players are prone to underestimate the importance as well as the intrinsic interest of the endgame stage. The wealth of instructive endgame play presented here will give the reader a rewarding glimpse into the artistry and practical value of the endgame.

My object then has been to make every page count. Superfluities and side issues have been avoided. In this way, I hope, the book genuinely lives up to its title.

East Meadow, N. Y.   FRED REINFELD
January 1961

CONTENTS

HOW TO PLAY BETTER CHESS

CHAPTER I

The Basic Principle of Opening Play: Importance of the Center

Like most chessplayers, you have doubtless devoted years to more or less desultory study of the openings. But no matter how many variations you memorize, and no matter how well you remember them, the knowledge thus gained is virtually useless unless it is combined with an understanding of the center—its value and its importance.

What do we Mean by the Center?

The center is the complex of squares which includes K3, Q3, KB4, K4, Q4, QB4, KB5, K5, Q5, QB5, K6 and Q6.

THE CENTER

The important Pawns (see the area enclosed by the heavy line on the accompanying diagram) are therefore the King's Pawn, the Queen's Pawn, the King's Bishop's Pawn and the Queen's Bishop's Pawn. As a rule only the King's Pawn and the Queen's Pawn are called "center Pawns." The Bishops' Pawns are of subordinate importance for two reasons:

(1) When placed at the fourth rank, the King's Pawn and the Queen's Pawn command *two squares* in the center. The Bishops' Pawns, at the fourth rank,

3

command only *one square* in the center. We shall see later on that the center squares are the strongest, the most valuable, and the most important squares on the board. Hence the King's Pawn and Queen's Pawn are more valuable than the Bishops' Pawns.

(2) The advance of the King's Pawn and the Queen's Pawn opens up more avenues of development than does the advance of the Bishops' Pawns. Since we want to develop quickly and effectively, the role of the King's Pawn and Queen's Pawn naturally takes on added importance.

Why is the Center Important?

The center is important because (other things being equal):

(1) A piece placed in the center (especially K_4, K_5, Q_4, or Q_5) is posted where it can exert its maximum efficiency. You can test this easily and convincingly by counting the number of squares commanded by a Queen, a Bishop or a Knight when placed at K_5, KB_5, or KR_1.

From this important feature of the center, we deduce the principle that:

(2) Pieces placed in the center can easily be transferred from one part of the center to another; also that pieces placed in the center *can readily be switched to either wing.*

To get some practical value from these principles, we may observe that a player *who has a strong grip on the center* has excellent chances of success if he undertakes an attack against an opponent *who has an infirm hold (or none at all) on the center.* Conversely, a player *who has only slight command of the center* is inviting disaster if he attacks a player *who controls the center.*

Stated in abstract form, as these principles usually are, they make very little impression on the imagination and learning faculties of the inexperienced player. We shall therefore proceed to study concrete examples, with the caution that general rules cannot apply to occasional extraordinary positions; although it is hardly conceivable that a player who does not command the center could arrive at a powerful attacking formation.

White to move

(Copenhagen, 1933)

NIMZOVICH

ENEVOLDSEN

The diagrammed position shows a powerful attack based on complete control of the center. White's forces are posted aggressively for King-side attack. Black's pieces are exiled from the center; they are divided and ineffectual. There followed:

1 R×Kt!!   B×R
2 Kt–R5   Kt–Kt3
3 Kt(4)–B6ch! K–R1

Now we see why Black's Bishop was deflected from the King-side. If ... P×Kt; 4 Kt×Pch, K–Kt2; 5 Q–R5 forces mate.

4 Kt×KtP!!   R–KKt1

If 4 ... K×Kt; 5 Q–R5 etc.

5 Kt×RP!!   K×Kt(Kt2)

On 5 ... R×Kt; 6 Kt–B6 leads to a mating attack.

6 Q–R5   P–B4
7 P×P e.p. *ch* K–B2
8 Kt–Kt5ch   K×P
9 Q–B3ch   K–K2
10 Q–B7ch   K–Q1
11 Q×Rch and wins

Another convincing instance of a devastating attack based on complete control of the center appears in the game Forgacs—Cohn (page 48).

An example of the reverse principle (attacking with inadequate control of the center) is seen in the following play:

[See diagram on p. 6.]

1 Q–R5?   P–KR3
2 P–B4   Kt–Q2
3 P–K4   P–K4!

An embarrassing problem for White: after 4 P×P he will be left with an isolated King's Pawn, and he will never be able to drive away any piece which Black posts on K4. On the other hand, if White advances 4 P–B5, then

White to move

(Berlin, 1928)

CAPABLANCA

MARSHALL

Black operates on the Queen's file, where he has a powerful *outpost* at Q5. (This square is a *hole*—it is not commanded by any White Pawns, and is therefore ideally suited for occupation by Black pieces. The term *outpost* is explained on p. 21.)

If White gives up his attacking policy, he will have to spend time bringing his *decentralized* Queen back into play. He will also have trouble defending his *backward* King's Pawn. Hence he decides to continue his attack at all cost.

| 4 Kt–B3 | QR–K1 |
| 5 Kt–R4 | |

Another piece removed from the center! The threat of Kt–B5 is easily met by Black.

| 5 .... | P×P! |
| 6 R×P | Q–Kt4! |

Forcing White to retreat (7 Q×Q? loses a piece).

| 7 Q–B3 | Kt–K4 |

Occupying a beautiful central post with gain of time.

| 8 Q–B2 | Kt×B |

Destroying the protection of the King's Pawn.

| 9 R×Kt | R×P |

White has a lost game; he resigned 12 moves later.

Developing at the Opponent's Expense

Neglect of the center by one side generally enables the opponent to develop with gain of time. This is often seen in the games of inexperienced players. Here is an example which is impressive by reason of its very simplicity:

VIENNA GAME

Nuremberg, 1889

WHITE	BLACK
M. Kurschner	S. Tarrasch

1 P-K4	P-K4
2 Kt-QB3	Kt-KB3
3 B-B4	Kt×P!
4 B×P*ch?*	

This game is instructive because it is played by a fair amateur against one of the greatest masters that ever lived; the contrast is a violent one!

The text is the kind of move which is almost irresistible for a player ignorant of *positional* considerations: it is "brilliant," and it prevents Black from castling. But for all that, it is a shallow move. This "sacrifice," as the master of course knows, is a transaction (and a highly unprofitable one at that) whereby White loses the *more important* King's Pawn for the *less valuable* King's Bishop Pawn. The Black King is perfectly safe, since White's limited possibilities of development preclude his obtaining an attack worthy of the name.

4	K×B
5 Kt×Kt	P-Q4
6 Q-B3*ch*	K-Kt1
7 Kt-K2	B-K3

Not 7 ... P×Kt*??*; 8 Q-Kt3*ch* and mate follows!

8 Kt(4)-Kt3	Kt-B3
9 P-QR3	Q-Q2
10 P-R3	B-QB4

Black's advantage is colossal. His mighty center and the steady development of his pieces with gain of time smother White's game. The immediate threat is 11 ... R-KB1 (ungratefully *utilizing the King's Bishop file* which White has opened for him!).

| 11 O-O | P-KR4 |

Hemming in White's position still more: the Knight at Kt3 has no good square (K4 is taken away from him by Black's *center Pawn* at Q4), and 12 Kt×P? is answered by 12 ... R-KB1 winning the Knight.

| 12 Kt-R1 | R-KB1 |

13 Q–KKt3 P–R5
14 Q–R2   P–K5
15 P–Q3

At last he essays a timid advance in the center—but the game is over!

[See diagram, next column.]

15 ....   B–Q3
16 B–B4   R × B!
17 Kt × R   P–KKt4
  Resigns

He must lose the Knight at KB4, and his position is hopeless.

This game, with its feeble play by White, has been purposely selected to illustrate *the dire results of neglecting the center.*

Exploitation of Weaknesses Arising from Lack of Mobility

There are some Pawn center formations which are so powerful that the opponent is unable to get his fair share of the center, and is thus deprived of mobility for his pieces. The following position is a case in point.

White's *well-supported center* is all-powerful. Black's Bishop and Knight have no mobility to speak of. The freeing moves ... P–K4 and ... P–QB4 have been restrained, at least for some time to come. As the game goes on, Black's game is likely to become more and more *constricted*.

When a player finds himself in a situation like the above, his prospects are bleak indeed. He must try to gain ground in the center. If such a course is impossible, he must resign himself to passive defense (a very distasteful alternative) or else he must strike out in any way he can to achieve freedom. In that event, he is likely to create weaknesses which lend themselves readily to exploitation by an opponent who has greater maneuvering freedom. An instructive example of this process appears in the following game:

QUEEN'S GAMBIT
DECLINED

St. Petersburg, 1909

WHITE	BLACK
A.	*C.*
Rubinstein	*Schlechter*
1 P–Q4	P–Q4
2 Kt–KB3	Kt–KB3
3 P–B4	P–K3
4 B–Kt5	B–K2
5 Kt–B3	QKt–Q2
6 P–K3	P–B3
7 B–Q3	P×P
8 B×BP	Kt–Q4

Black is following a well-known system of defense in this opening. With his seventh move he "gave up the center"—that is, he relinquished the control over White's K4 which he had previously exercised with his Queen's Pawn. The idea of this defensive system appears with the text:

simplification, after which Black will be able to recover a satisfactory share of the center.

9 B×B	Q×B
10 O–O	O–O
11 R–B1	

Black's difficulty, be it noted, is a two-fold one: (1) his Bishop is hemmed in, and (2) his K4 and QB4 may fall under White's control. The exchange transaction 11 ... Kt×Kt; 12 R×Kt, P–K4! would remove both difficulties.

White's Queen's Pawn would then disappear (unless he reconciled himself to an isolated Queen's Pawn, in which case Black could still develop his Bishop without any difficulty). The squares K4 and QB4 would become available to Black's Knight if White recaptured on Q4 (after ... $P \times P$) with a piece. If White answered ... $P \times P$ with $P \times P$, then Black could bring his Knight to the excellent post Q4.

11 ....   R–Q1

Pointless, although it still does not spoil anything.

12 Q–B2   Kt–B1?

But this is bad: *the Knight must be in the center or its vicinity. As it approaches the edge of the board, its powers diminish perceptibly.*

The voluntary (!) retreat of the Knight deprives it of any influence in the center. At the same time the vital advance ... P–K4 becomes impossible.

13 P–K4   Kt–QKt3?

A second strategical blunder. This Knight will have no scope *at the side of the board,* and it cannot return to the center, as *the square Q4 is now commanded by the White King's Pawn.*

13 ... $Kt \times Kt$ was the logical move.

14 B–Kt3   B–Q2?

Worse and worse: there was still a chance for Black by playing ... P–QB4, in order *to liquidate White's Queen's Pawn, with its control of K5 and QB5.*

15 Kt–K2!

The lid is clamped down tightly. Now ... P–K4 and ... P–QB4 are impossible.

15 ....   B–K1
16 KR–Q1   QR–B1

The consequence of Black's neglect of the center is that his Bishop has no good squares, his Rooks have little scope, and the Knights are wretchedly placed.

But White cannot afford to rest on his laurels. *The advantage in space can be maintained (or*

converted into a different advantage) only by unremitting vigilance.

In the present position, for example, Black threatens to play one of his Knights to Q2, after which he can force either ... P–K4 or ... P–QB4. But Rubinstein is on his guard and plays:

17 Q–B3!   R–B2

If 17 ... Kt(1)–Q2; 18 Q–R5!, P–QR3; 19 Kt–Kt3, P–QB4 (19 ... P–K4 is obviously not feasible); 20 P×P, R×P; 21 R×R and wins.

18 Kt–B4   P–B3

The first serious weakness, induced by Black's anxiety to give his Bishop a new diagonal.

19 Q–R5

A well-timed diversion: if 19 ... Kt–B1; 20 Kt×P!.

19 ....   P–Kt4

This opens the gate to the enemy, but Black has no other way to save the King's Pawn. The first weakness has led to a second weakness!

20 Kt–K2   Kt–B1

21 P–Q5!!

In view of the disorganized state of Black's game, this move is decisive.

21 ....   R(2)–Q2

He has no good reply, for example 21 ... P–Kt3; 22 Q–B3, KP×P (or 22 ... B–B2; 23 Kt[2]–Q4, KP×P; 24 Kt–B5, Q×P; 25 Q×KBP, Kt–K3; 26 Kt×P and wins); 23 KP×P!, Q×Kt; 24 P–Q6*ch*, R–B2; 25 Q×KBP, R–Q2; 26 R–K1, Q–Kt4; 27 R×B, Q×B; 28 Q×P*ch* and wins.

22	Kt(2)–Q4	BP×P
23	P×P	R×P

The exchange cannot be saved: if 23 ... B–B2 (or 23 ... P×P; 24 B–R4, P–Kt3; 25 Q–R6, R–B2; 26 Kt–B5 etc.);

24 R–K1, P–K4; 25 Kt–B5, Q–K1; 26 B–R4 etc.

24	B×R	R×B
25	Q–K1!	

And White won through the advantage of the exchange.

The Significance of Pawn Exchanges in the Center

Exchanges of Pawns in the center are an objective feature of chess play. They take place whether or not we realize their significance. As we shall see, it is of the greatest importance to be aware of the effect that a seemingly harmless exchange of Pawns may have on the further course of the game.

Pawn Exchanges Resulting in an Open File

This type is perhaps the most important of all, for the resulting open line may be of key importance to the whole future course of the game.

GRUENFELD DEFENSE
Lodz, 1935

WHITE	BLACK
S. Tartakover	A. Frydman

1	P–Q4	Kt–KB3
2	P–QB4	P–KKt3
3	Kt–QB3	P–Q4
4	B–B4	P–B3
5	P–K3	B–Kt2
6	Q–Kt3	O–O
7	Kt–B3	P×P
8	B×P	P–QKt4
9	B–K2	B–K3

10	Q–B2	Kt–Q4
11	Kt×Kt!	P×Kt

An interesting position.

I. THE PROBLEM

An inexperienced player might dismiss this position as about even, because both players have access to the Queen's Bishop file, with a likelihood of exchange of the Rooks. As a matter of actual fact, White's positional advantage is so marked that it is not an exaggeration to say that even at this early stage, White has a won game! What are the reasons for this drastic judgment?

THE BLACK BISHOPS. Both Black Bishops are passive: the King's Bishop stares at a stone wall (the more than securely protected White Queen's Pawn) and has no effect whatever on the state of the long diagonal. Worse yet, this Bishop has no prospect of being shifted to the Queen-side, where the real action will take place. The only way that such a shift could be accomplished would be by moving away the Queen's Bishop, playing ... P–K3 and ... R–K1 and ... B–KB1. Needless to say, there is no time for such fantastically cumbersome maneuvers.

But Black's other Bishop is likewise in a bad way. It is blocked by its own Queen's Pawn, to whose defense it is practically tied, as we shall see later. But even if the Bishop were free to leave K3, it would have no good square at its disposal. True, KB4 would not be a bad post; but occupation of the square is meaningless of itself unless effective cooperation with the other pieces is possible.

THE WHITE BISHOPS. Here we have a totally different situation. White's Queen's Bishop is not enclosed by a chain of Pawns, nor does it confront a stone wall. It is directed right at Black's vulnerable Queen-side. Consider, especially, the effect of a possible White occupation of QB7 with one of his Rooks. So powerful, in fact, is this "harmless bystander" role of the Bishop that it may play a vital part in the remaining phase *without making another move!*

The other White Bishop is also performing a useful function. At this moment, to be sure, B × P? would be a blunder because of ... Q–R4ch; but this tactical finesse will vanish shortly, and then Black will find himself in serious difficulties because of the weakness of his Queen's Knight Pawn.

DEVELOPMENT. Here White has a clear advantage: not only are his Bishops better developed in a *qualitative* sense, but his Knight is already out, whereas his Black colleague is still at home. Furthermore, White can get a Rook to the Queen's Bishop file in one move, whereas Black needs two moves for the same purpose. This circumstance, coupled with White's observation of QB7, gives us a valuable hint: it is very likely that White will be able to control the all-important Queen's Bishop file.

PAWN POSITION. Still another point in White's favor: whereas his Pawn position is quite free from weaknesses, Black's formation shows a hideous flaw, the advanced Queen's Knight Pawn. Not only is the advanced Pawn a target for White's attack; the advance of the Queen's Pawn and Queen's Knight Pawn has left Black's QB4 a *hole* constantly subject to the threat of occupation.

To conclude: there can be little doubt that White has a strategically won game. His Bishops operate effectively while Black's Bishops are hemmed in; White is also ahead in development; he will be the first to occupy the Queen's Bishop file; he has no Pawn weaknesses or weak squares, while Black is weak in both respects. All these

factors will make themselves felt very quickly.

II. THE SOLUTION

12 O–O   Q–Kt3

After 12 ... P–QR3; 13 P–QR4! Black would be in trouble. The text also has the objective of clearing the last rank, so that Black's Rooks can get to QB1 as rapidly as possible.

13 Q–Kt3!

Without loss of time White makes room for moving his Rooks to the Queen's Bishop file.

13 ....   P–Kt5

13 ... P–QR3; 14 P–QR4, P–Kt5; 15 P–R5, Q–Kt2; 16 KR–B1, Kt–B3; 17 R–B5 leads to a similar position.

14 KR–B1   Kt–B3

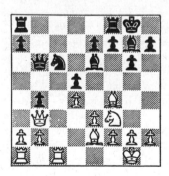

15 R–B5!

Occupying the vulnerable square. White now threatens to win a Pawn with 16 B–QKt5.

15 .... KR–B1

Or 15 ... QR–B1; 16 QR–QB1, P–QR4; 17 Q–R4, Kt–R2; 18 R × R, Kt × R (if 18 ... R × R?; 19 R × Rch followed by 20 Q–K8ch leads to mate); 19 R–B5 winning a Pawn.

16 QR–QB1 P–QR4
17 Q–R4!

The pressure on the Queen's Bishop file has become intolerable, for if 17 ... B–Q2?; 18 B–QKt5 wins.

17 .... Kt–R2
18 R × Rch B × R

Or 18 ... R × R; 19 R × Rch, B × R; 20 Q–K8ch, B–B1; 21 B–KR6 followed by mate.

19 Q–K8ch B–B1

Now 20 B–KR6? would be refuted by 20 ... B–Kt2.

[See diagram, next column.]

20 Kt–Kt5

Winning a Pawn. Note the horribly disorganized state of Black's pieces!

20 .... Q–KB3
21 Kt × RP Q–Kt2

Equally dreary would be 21 ... K × Kt; 22 Q × B and Black has nothing better than 22 ... Q–Kt2 in view of the threat of 23 B–K5 (if 22 ... Kt–B3; 23 R × Kt, Q × R; 24 Q × Pch etc.).

22 Q × Bch Q × Q
23 Kt × Q K × Kt
24 R–B5 Resigns

Black's position is in ruins, and he must lose a second Pawn.

Pawn Exchanges Resulting in Weaknesses

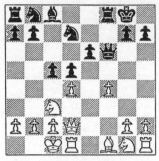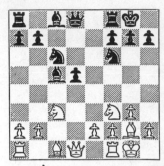

FRENCH DEFENSE   QUEEN'S GAMBIT DECLINED

Another significant aspect of Pawn exchanges is the way in which they sometimes give rise to weaknesses. For example: 1 P–K4, P–K3; 2 P–Q4, P–Q4; 3 Kt–QB3, Kt–KB3; 4 B–Kt5, B–K2; 5 P–K5, KKt–Q2; 6 B×B, Q×B; 7 Q–Q2, O–O; 8 P–B4, P–QB4; 9 O–O–O, P–B3 (the natural line of play: Black must obtain freedom for his rather cramped pieces); 10 KP×P, Q×P. Result of the Pawn exchanges: a backward King's Pawn for Black.

A further example from the Queen's Gambit Declined: 1 P–Q4, P–Q4; 2 P–QB4, P–K3; 3 Kt–QB3, P–QB4; 4 BP×P, KP×P; 5 Kt–B3, Kt–QB3; 6 P–KKt3!, Kt–B3; 7 B–Kt2, B–K2; 8 O–O, O–O; 9 P×P!, B×P. Black is left with an isolated Queen's Pawn on which White can train his guns.

For the treatment of such a weakness, see the game Reinfeld —Horowitz, page 35.

Pawn Exchanges Resulting in Half-open Files

This type of exchange is of far greater importance than the amateur generally realizes, because of the far-reaching strategical considerations which are often involved. For example:

1 P–Q4	P–Q4
2 P–QB4	P–K3
3 Kt–QB3	Kt–KB3
4 B–Kt5	B–K2
5 P–K3	QKt–Q2
6 Kt–B3	O–O
7 R–B1	P–B3
8 Q–B2	R–K1
9 P×P	KP×P

Here we have one of the most frequently recurring positions in the Queen's Gambit Declined. White has a half-open Queen's Bishop file, Black has a half-open King's file. White will attempt to establish one of his Knights as an *outpost* at QB5; he may also attempt to undermine Black's position with P–QKt4–5.

Black will attempt to establish his King's Knight as an *outpost* at K5, and he may reinforce it with ... P–KB4. White will attack on the Queen-side, Black on the King-side. And all these manifold possibilities arise from the exchange of Pawns in the center!

One of the best possible ways to improve your play is to set up positions at about the tenth move and see what you can forecast about the future course of the game.

Removing the Tension in the Pawn Center

As we have observed, center Pawns are very often so posted that they can be exchanged for each other. As the exchanges may lead to different kinds of games (through the opening of files) a player will often dispel the tension (rob the position of its elasticity or uncertainty) by brusquely removing the possibility of Pawn exchanges. Here is an enlightening example:

*QUEEN'S GAMBIT
DECLINED*

Berlin, 1935

WHITE	BLACK
F. Saemisch	*H. Taube*
1 P–Q4	P–Q4
2 P–QB4	P–K3
3 Kt–QB3	P–QB4
4 BP×P	KP×P
5 Kt–B3	Kt–QB3
6 P–KKt3	Kt–B3
7 B–Kt2	

Up to this point there is tension in the center: White's Queen's Pawn and Black's Queen's Bishop Pawn are mutually *en prise*. "Suppose," you may ask, "that from this point the game continues with 7 ... P–B5. Then White can no longer isolate the hostile Queen's Pawn. What has he gained?

"How does play continue?"

It is a reasonable query. For Black is relieved to a certain extent of the weakness of his Queen's Pawn, and he has the advantage (for the endgame) of three Pawns to two on the Queen-side.

However, 7 ... P–B5 *does* have a definite drawback: *it removes the tension in the center* (the Pawns are no longer mutually *en prise*). The result is that White's grip on K5 is greatly intensified, since his Queen's Pawn, the main support of this hold on K5, *is no longer menaced by a possible exchange for Black's Queen's Bishop Pawn.*

The logical course for White, therefore, is to concentrate on K5. And so play continues:

7	P–B5*?!*
8 O–O	B–K2
9 B–Kt5*!*	

Undermining the support of the Queen's Pawn, which is still weak because *it cannot be supported by Pawns and must be guarded by pieces.*

9	B–K3
10 R–B1	O–O
11 Kt–K5*!*	Q–Kt3

Black's prospects seem excellent, because of the double

attack on White's Queen's Pawn and Queen's Knight Pawn. Yet White, relying on his command of K5 (note that Black cannot exchange Knights without losing a piece), calmly plays:

12 P–K3!   QR–Q1

He admits that his Queen's Pawn is weak after all! If 12 ... Q×KtP; 13 P–B4, QR–Q1; 14 P–B5, B–B1; 15 B×Kt, B×B; 16 Kt–Kt4, Kt–K2; 17 Kt×Bch, P×Kt; 18 R–QB2, Q–Kt3; 19 Q–R5 and Black discovers that he has salvaged his Queen's Pawn only at the cost of provoking a mighty attack.

13 P–B4   Q–R4

To give the Queen's Pawn additional protection.

14 P–B5   B–B1

15 B×Kt   B×B
16 Kt–Kt4

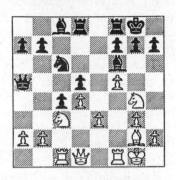

16 ....   Kt–K2

Black's position is hopeless: if 16 ... B–K2; 17 P–B6!, B×Kt?; 18 Q×B winning a piece!

17 Kt×Bch   P×Kt
18 Q–R5   K–R1
19 R–B4

The attack plays itself.

19 ....   Kt–Kt1
20 QR–KB1   KR–K1
21 R–R4   P–KR3
22 R(1)–B4   R×P
23 R(B4)–Kt4

Threatens 24 Q×Pch!.

23 ....   B×P
24 R×Ktch!   Resigns

White has played very cleverly.

The French Defense abounds in examples of the importance of tension in the center. In the Saemisch—Taube game we saw how a player may expose himself to a vicious attack by removing the tension; the French Defense offers many examples of how a player may *lose his advantage* by premature removal of the tension.

Thus, after 1 P–K4, P–K3; 2 P–Q4, P–Q4 White has an advantage in space; but by playing 3 P × P, P × P (the tension is gone) he reduces the game to a dreary symmetrical position whose chief feature is unutterable boredom.

Hence White usually defends his King's Pawn (after 1 P–K4, P–K3; 2 P–Q4, P–Q4) with 3 Kt–QB3. If Black relieves the tension in the center now with 3 ... P × P; 4 Kt × P, he manifestly yields some terrain in the center to White. While this line is playable (although not inviting) for Black, the usual course is 3 ... Kt–KB3, whereby Black renews his attack on the King's Pawn and still maintains the tension.

Now White's choice of a reply is fairly circumscribed:

(1) 4 P × P, P × P again removes the tension and leads to a dull, approximately even game.

(2) 4 B–Q3 allows 4 ... P–B4! followed by Pawn exchanges which will facilitate Black's development.

(3) 4 P–K5 again relieves the tension, so that after 4 ... KKt–Q2 Black is ready to counter successfully with ... P–QB4.

(4) 4 B–Kt5—the usual move—which keeps up the tension in the center.

The opening still abounds in a variety of problems for both players, but we shall take leave of it here, as we have already noted seven examples of the importance of maintaining the tension.

One last comment: the player who has the advantage should never release the tension prematurely. The reason for this is that where the center is *mobile*, the position is *elastic*: it permits of the adoption of two or more alternative plans of procedure depending on the ultimate disposition of the center Pawns. This is likely to be extremely inconvenient for the player with the inferior game, as he must always reckon with the possibility of having to defend himself on several fronts. On the other hand, an early exchange of Pawns will automatically rule out certain lines of play, thus simplifying the defender's task. Even where the defender's task is fairly difficult, it comes to him as a great relief to know that he is menaced in only one specific way.

Pivot Points and Outposts

These are made possible by certain types of Pawn exchanges. Thus, in the French Defense, after the moves 1 P–K4, P–K3; 2 P–Q4, P–Q4; 3 Kt–QB3, P×P; 4 Kt×P we have a "half-center" made up of White's Pawn at Q4 and Black's Pawn at K3. White's K4 and Black's Q4 are *pivot points* (squares which are valuable links of communication for one's pieces).

White's K5 is not only a *pivot point*; it is also an admirable square for an *outpost* (a piece which occupies an advanced square in an open or half-open file, and is supported by a Pawn). The piece most frequently utilized as an outpost is the Knight, which is placed to great advantage in this capacity.

In many openings (such as the Ruy Lopez, Sicilian Defense, Philidor's Defense, etc.) there are variations in which there are "half-centers" made up of a White Pawn at K4 and a Black Pawn at Q3. Here (analogous to the example given from the French Defense) White's Q4 and Black's K4 are *pivot points*; White's Q5 is both a *pivot point* and an admirable square for an *outpost*.

The following game will show us the practical utility of pivot points and outposts:

KING'S INDIAN DEFENSE

The Hague, 1928

WHITE	BLACK
Dr. M. Euwe	*C. Carls*
1 Kt–KB3	Kt–KB3
2 P–B4	P–B4
3 P–KKt3	Kt–B3
4 B–Kt2	P–KKt3
5 P–Kt3	B–Kt2
6 B–Kt2	P–Q3
7 P–Q4	P×P
8 Kt×P	B–Q2
9 O–O	O–O

The exchange after 7 P–Q4 has resulted in a half-center (White Pawn at QB4, Black Pawn at Q3), in which White has three pivot points (Q4, K4 and Q5) and a square for an outpost (Q5); while Black has one square (K4) which might theoretically be available as a pivot point.

Before you proceed with the game, you will find it useful to remember that *pieces are posted with maximum efficiency in the center.* Utilizing outposts and pivot points automatically gives one's pieces effective spheres of operation.

| 10 Kt–QB3 | Kt×Kt |

Carls hopes to minimize his opponent's greater command of the board by simplifying exchanges.

| 11 Q×Kt | B–B3 |
| 12 Kt–Q5! | |

The outpost!

12	Kt–R4
13 Q–Q2	B×B
14 Q×B	B×Kt

Ridding himself of the outpost, which hampers the movements of Black's pieces too much. This undertaking is not an unqualified success: his remaining Knight is inferior to White's Bishop, which is so splendidly posted on the long diagonal. In addition, White has a fine basis of operations on the half-open Queen file.

| 15 B×B | |

Here we have a fine example of the power of a *centralized* piece. The Bishop is beautifully posted on Q5 (trained on KB7 *and* QKt7). Its strength derives from the fact that it is an outpost, while at the same time it is placed on a pivot point.

| 15 .... | Q–Kt3 |
| 16 KR–Q1 | Kt–B3 |

Driving away the Bishop (the latter being the stronger piece, White is naturally loath to exchange); but the Knight's position proves unexpectedly vulnerable.

| 17 B–B3 | KR–B1 |

Threatens ... R × P.

| 18 R–Q4 | P–QR4 |
| 19 QR–Q1 | R–B2 |

His position is difficult. If he tries ... K–Kt2 (to give his

Knight more protection), then 20 P–KKt4 is very troublesome.

| 20 P–KR4 | P–R4 |

Weakening his King-side and thereby allowing an ingenious combination.

21 R × P*!*

An accurately calculated sacrifice of the exchange, which will be more than compensated for by two Pawns, the centralized Bishop at Q5 and the occupation of KB6.

Note in the play that follows that Black's pieces, being concentrated on the Queen-side, can be brought to the threatened sector only with the greatest difficulty; while White, with his occupation of the Queen's file and particularly the pivot point Q5, brings up new forces to the attack with alarming swiftness: an example of how *command of the*

*center makes it possible to shift
one's pieces rapidly.*

| 21 .... | P×R |
| 22 Q×Kt | R–KB1 |

He cannot hold the feeble
Queen's Pawn. Thus if 22 ...
R–Q2; 23 B–Q5!, K–R2; 24
B×BP—or 22 ... R–R3; 23
B–Q5!, K–B1; 24 R–Q3 fol-
lowed by 25 R–K3, winning
easily in either case.

| 23 R×P | Q–B4 |
| 24 B–Q5! | K–R2 |

White menaced 25 Q×KtP*ch*.

| 25 P–KKt4! | Q–R6 |

The only way to bring the
Queen to the defense; but it is
futile all the same. If instead 25
... P×P; 26 P–R5 decides.

26 P×P	Q–B8*ch*
27 K–R2	Q–R3
28 B×BP!	Q–Kt2

If either Rook captures the
Bishop, then 29 P×P*ch*, K–Kt1;
30 P×R*ch* wins the Queen!

| 29 P×P*ch* | K–R1 |
| 30 Q–Kt5 | *Resigns* |

This smartly played game by
Euwe is a masterly illustration of
the use of a pivot point, outpost
and the half-open file.

How Outposts Provoke Exchanges

In some positions, the outpost may be so strongly entrenched
that the opponent has no choice, and must remove it despite
the fact that the exchange is disadvantageous for other reasons.
Two cases in point:

NIMZOVICH

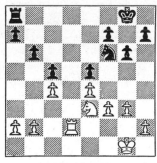

CAPABLANCA

White to move

(New York, 1927)

White should play 1 R–Q6!,
K–Kt2 (if the Knight moves,
then 2 R–Q7 and White's command of the seventh rank should
suffice for victory); 2 Kt–Q5!

Now Black has an unpleasant
choice between 2 ... Kt×Kt;
3 KP×Kt, K–B1; 4 R–Q7
(when White's command of the
seventh rank, plus his protected

passed Pawn, should assure the win); or 2 ... Kt–K1; 3 R–Q7 (when the command of the seventh rank, plus White's magnificent posting of the Knight at Q5, leaves Black with a lost game).

[See diagram, next column.]

In order to obtain some maneuvering room for his pieces, Black must sooner or later remove the obnoxious Knight. He plays ... B×Kt, but after the reply BP×B a new difficulty arises: he is left with a weak Queen's Bishop Pawn, on which White can train both Rooks and the Queen as well. Thus we see how

Black to move

(Zurich, 1934)

JOHNER

FLOHR

the advantage of the outpost has been converted into a new advantage: pressure on a weak Pawn.

How Outposts Provoke Pawn Weaknesses

The establishment of an outpost sometimes has a more than merely logical and analytically demonstrable function: it has a psychological value. The opponent becomes irritated at the presence of the intruder and is determined to be rid of him at all cost, even if the expulsion results in a permanent weakness.

We have already had a foretaste of this type of strategy in the previous example (Flohr—Johner). The provoking of weaknesses in this manner is one of the great achievements of the positional method of playing chess: first constrict your opponent's position; then provoke weaknesses in his game; finally, exploit the newly created weaknesses.

Black to move

(Nuremberg, 1910)

VOGEL

TARRASCH

In his haste to be rid of the outpost, Black plays:

1 ....   P–QB3?

True, ... R–B1? is refuted by 2 Kt–K7*ch*. But preferable to the text was 1 ... Kt–B3 (if 2 Kt×P, QR–B1 regains the Pawn).

2 Kt–K7*ch*   K–R1

Black is left with a permanent weakness on Q3 as a result of his

driving off the Knight.

3 Kt–B5   QR–Q1
4 QR–Q1   P–KKt3
5 Kt–Q6   R–Q2

Note that *both* the Queen's Knight Pawn and the King's Bishop Pawn were threatened!

6 P–B5!

Another consequence of 1 ... P–QB3? One White Pawn paralyzes three Black Pawns.

6 ....   K–Kt1
7 Kt–B4!   KR–Q1

If 7 ... R–K2, White doubles Rooks on the Queen's file and wins rather easily.

8 R×R   R×R
9 P–B3   Kt–R3
10 Kt×P   R–Q7
11 Kt–B4   R–QB7
12 P–QKt3   R×P
13 R–Q1!   P–R4
14 R–Q8*ch*   K–Kt2
15 R–QR8

White won easily.

In Conclusion

You have now had many examples of the importance of the center; of the ways in which to secure and maintain its control; of its relation to attack and defense; of the most effective ways to post pieces in the center; of the value of the center for communication between the wings; of the significance of central Pawn exchanges.

This new knowledge of the center will prove useful to you in future study of the openings, and in reading the next three chapters on middle game play. Again and again you will observe that the middle game proceeds on lines determined by the center formation of the previous opening play.

CHAPTER II

Problems of the Middle Game:
The Fine Art of Strategical Play

In this and the next two chapters you will be able to apply much of the knowledge gained in Chapter I; for the transactions that have taken place in the center foreshadow the kind of play that will appear in the middle game.

The subject of strategy, as treated here, comprises for the most part the proper methods of operating against hostile weaknesses. The chief lesson you are to learn here is that there is a vast gap between *attacking* and *defending*; between *choosing* to exploit a weakness and *being forced* to defend it.

We shall see the same contrast between maneuvering with ample mobility, on the one hand, and being constrained to make passive defensive maneuvers in a constricted position.

Whenever possible, seize the initiative; hold it; make good use of it!

The Pawn Center as a Liability!

Much of what we have learned about the center has been derived from the teachings of Tarrasch. To him, the center was definitely a *Pawn center*. He rained down maledictions on what he considered the terrible blunder of "giving up the center" (exchanging King's Pawn or Queen's Pawn for an enemy Bishop's Pawn).

In due course the Hypermoderns, particularly Nimzovich and Breyer, stood Tarrasch's theory on its head and proclaimed that the Pawn center was a conveniently vulnerable target at the enemy's mercy! Infuriated by Tarrasch's doctrinaire assertion that "cramped positions carry within themselves the germ of defeat," his opponents replied with equally absurd fanaticism.

The reasonable observations on this controversy are: (1) The Pawn center may be *either* an asset or a liability. (2) In each case we must judge the Pawn center on its merits.

In the following game an apparently powerful Pawn center turns out to be weak. Nevertheless the writer hazards a sly suspicion that if Nimzovich had had the White pieces, the White Pawn center would have turned out to be a tower of strength! So this cynical thought gives us one more conclusion: (3) Pawn centers are strong or weak depending on the uses to which they are put.

	OLD-INDIAN	13 P–B4	Kt–Kt3
	DEFENSE		
	Ostend, 1907		

WHITE	BLACK
H. Shoosmith	*A. Nimzovich*
1 P–Q4	Kt–KB3
2 P–QB4	P–Q3
3 Kt–KB3	QKt–Q2
4 Kt–B3	P–K4
5 P–K4	B–K2
6 B–Q3	O–O
7 O–O	P × P!?
8 Kt × P	R–K1
9 P–QKt3	Kt–K4
10 B–B2	P–QR3
11 B–Kt2	B–Q2
12 P–KR3	B–KB1

One's first impression is that White has an overwhelming position—"all the consequence," Tarrasch would add triumphantly, "of Black's surrender of the center on move 7."

But Nimzovich sees his compensations: by surrendering the center, he obtained K4 as an outpost. To deprive him of this asset, White played P–B4, driving away Black's Knight and getting a really imposing center. The consequence is, however, that White's King's Pawn is under some pressure and can no longer be protected by a Pawn.

Note also that while Black's position is somewhat cramped, *his pieces have ample maneuvering space.*

14 Q–B3 P–B3

Now White is deprived of the use of Q5 as an outpost. His position looks good, but it is difficult for him to hit on a far-reaching plan. Black's position looks bad, but, as we shall see, it is full of stored-up energy and improves from move to move.

15 QR–K1 P–Kt4!

Now Black has a Queen-side counter-offensive in motion. Meanwhile White is still reduced to portentous preparations: P–B5 is always answered by ... Kt–K4; and P–K5 is impossible.

16 Q–Q3 Q–B2
17 K–R1 QR–Q1
18 B–Kt1

Still preparing . . . for what?!

18 .... P–Kt5!

Gaining further ground by assuring an unassailable post for a Knight at QB4.

19 Kt–Q1 B–B1

The elasticity of Nimzovich's maneuvering is very pleasing: the Bishop prepares to go to QKt2 (for the eventual grand liberating stroke ... P–Q4!!), and at the same time makes room for the transfer of the Knight from KB3 to QB4.

20 Q–KB3 Kt–Q2
21 Kt–B5 Kt–B4
22 P–Kt4?

Still trying to be aggressive, White commits the fatal blunder of opening up the diagonal on which both his King and Queen are placed.

22 .... Kt–K3
23 Q–Kt3 B–Kt2!

The Bishop is now on the right diagonal, and the air gets too rarefied for such a sensitive piece as White's King.

24 P–KR4   P–Q4!!

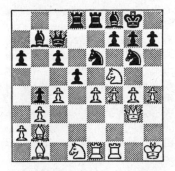

At last the long-awaited advance brings Black's bottled-up pieces to life. The advance is decisive, even though White has removed his Queen from the line of fire.

25 P–K5   P–B4!
26 P×P   R×P

Threatening a ferocious *discovered check*. 27 B–K4 will not help (27 ... R×Kt!). How bitterly White must regret his 22nd move!

27 K–Kt1   R–Q7
28 Kt(5)–K3

His other Knight is moveless because of the reply 28 ... R×B.

On 28 R–B2, KR–Q1 wins easily: Black has too many threats.

28 ....   Q–B3!
29 R–B3   Q×R
        Resigns

An unusually instructive game. White's Pawn center played a puny role.

Hypermodern Bishop vs. *Pawn Center*

In this game we see a struggle between two theories of the center. As far as Black is concerned, the good old views of Tarrasch are good enough for him: he simply plays out his center Pawns.

White, on the other hand, uses hypermodern strategy. He avoids moving either center Pawn at the beginning. His plan from the very start is to exert pressure on Q5, and even his "unmodern" advance of the Queen's Pawn is subordinate to this end.

To exert pressure on Q5, Reti plays 1 P–QB4 and strengthens his grip by fianchettoing his King's Bishop. In the end, his *strategy* triumphs only because he proves himself the better *tactician*!

ENGLISH OPENING

Marienbad, 1925

WHITE	BLACK
R. Reti	*D. Przepiorka*
1 P–QB4	Kt–KB3
2 Kt–QB3	P–K4
3 Kt–B3	Kt–B3
4 P–Q4	P×P
5 Kt×P	B–B4
6 Kt×Kt	KtP×Kt
7 P–KKt3	P–Q4
8 B–Kt2	B–K3
9 O–O	O–O

I. THE PROBLEM

White's task here is quite obvious: *maintenance of the pres-*

sure on the long diagonal. The idea of the exchange on the sixth move was of course to leave Black's Pawn position in a state that would render it highly vulnerable to the action of a Bishop fianchettoed at KKt2. White has already achieved this objective, with the result that Black's position is extremely uncomfortable.

This discomfort is all the more difficult to endure because it is permanent. The weakness of Black's Pawn position is such that it can never be eliminated or rendered less burdensome.

Let us be clear about the nature of this weakness: White's King's Bishop bears down on the hostile Queen's Pawn. The Pawn cannot move, for its advance would expose the pitiably weak Queen's Bishop Pawn, and would also open up new threats along the whole diagonal. Observe that whereas the Queen's Pawn at least has the support of the Queen's Bishop Pawn, the latter in turn has no *Pawn support* and has to be guarded by *pieces*.

To return to the Queen's

Pawn: since it cannot move, and since it is under continual fire by the enemy, it must be protected. But this leads to a new advantage for White: White's pieces *attack* the Queen's Pawn, while Black's pieces *defend* it. In other words, *White has the initiative.* He attacks the Queen's Pawn because he *wants to*; Black defends it because he *has to!*

So far the forces of attack and defense are fairly evenly balanced; but the outlook is dark for the defender. White can bring a new piece into the fight raging around the Queen's Pawn by playing B–Kt5. Furthermore, he can move his Queen and play a Rook to Q1, intensifying the pressure on Black's Pawns.

To sum up: White is in clover, as he has a clearly winning game. There is just one difficulty with which he may have to contend: he must be on guard against letting the defense get off too easily or obtaining some counter-play while White goes about his business of winning a Pawn. It frequently happens that the very moment of reaching the desired goal is just the time when the opponent gets a breathing spell and an opportunity to improve the position and thus lengthen his resistance.

It will be interesting to see how Reti avoids giving his opponent such a chance; *he wins the material without losing the initiative.*

II. THE SOLUTION

10 Q–R4*!*   B–Q2

He has no choice: if 10 ... Q–Q2?; 11 R–Q1, KR–Q1; 12 B–Kt5 and the Queen's Pawn is lost; or 10 ... P–Q5?; 11 Kt–K4 (or 11 R–Q1) winning a Pawn.

11 B–Kt5*!*

More pressure! 11 P × P? is premature, because after 11 ... P × P Black has time for ... P–B3 (supporting the center) because of the attack on White's Queen.

11 ....   B–K2
12 KR–Q1*!*   P–KR3

If 12 ... P–B4; 13 Q–R6 and the Queen's Pawn falls; or 12 ... P × P; 13 B × Kt, P × B; 14 B × P winning easily.

13 B × Kt   B × B

White must still be careful: if 14 P × P, P × P; 15 Q–R6, P–B3.

There is also a new difficulty: the coming cooperation of Black's

King's Bishop on the long diagonal and Black's Queen's Rook on the Queen's Knight file.

14 Q–R6!

Now there is a real threat of P×P. 14 ... P–Q5 is inadequate: 15 B×P!, P×Kt; 16 P×P!, B×P (or 16 ... Q–B1; 17 Q×Q); 17 QR–B1, Q–B1; 18 Q×Q etc.

14 ....   R–Kt1

So that if 15 R–Q2?, R×P!; 16 R×R, B×Kt; or 15 QR–Kt1, R–Kt3; 16 Q×P, Q–Kt1!

15 P×P!!   P×P

If 15 ... R×P or 15 ... B×Kt; 16 P×P! wins.

16 Kt×P   B×P

Or 16 ... R×P?; 17 Kt×Bch, P×Kt; 18 B–R3, R–Kt3; 19 Q×P, R–Q3; 20 R×R winning a piece!

17 QR–Kt1   P–QB3

If 17 ... B–Kt4; 18 Q×QRP, B×P; 19 R–Q2, B–B5; 20 R(2)×B, R×R; 21 R×R, B×Kt; 22 B×B, Q×B; 23 Q×P and White's extra Pawn wins.

18 Q×RP!

Continuing to play with admirable sharpness, Reti simplifies into an easily won position.

18	P×Kt
19 R×P	Q–K1
20 R×B	Q×P
21 R×P!	B–K4
22 R×R	R×R
23 R×Pch!	B×R
24 Q×Rch	K–R2
25 Q–Kt1ch	K–R1
26 B–K4	B–K4
27 Q–Kt7!	*Resigns*

Maneuvering against Positional Weaknesses

The difference between *defending* a weakness and *attacking* a weakness is the difference between being condemned to passivity and being privileged to enjoy the initiative.

A weakness is a hostage to fortune: the player who has a potential weakness must always worry about it; it gives him bleak prospects for the ending; his forces are deflected from constructively aggressive action.

Because the weakness also has a depressing effect, we often see games in which the opponent does not go after the weakness directly; he maneuvers more or less aimlessly, in cat-and-mouse fashion, to demonstrate that the weakness is permanent —that its possessor, even if not directly menaced and left to his own devices, can accomplish nothing of any value. Once this conviction sinks in, it is difficult indeed for the defender to offer stout resistance, and to take an unclouded view of the problems which he faces.

GRUENFELD DEFENSE

New York, 1932

WHITE	BLACK
F.	*I. A.*
Reinfeld	*Horowitz*
1 P–Q4	Kt–KB3
2 P–QB4	P–KKt3
3 Kt–QB3	P–Q4
4 P–K3	B–Kt2
5 Kt–B3	O–O
6 Q–Kt3	P–K3
7 B–Q2	P–Kt3
8 P×P	P×P
9 B–K2	B–Kt2
10 O–O	QKt–Q2

11 KR–Q1	P–B4?
12 P×P	Kt×P
13 Q–R3	Q–K2
14 B–K1	KR–Q1

By playing 11 ... P–B4?

(11 ... P–B3 was preferable) Black has chosen a move which conditions all the remaining play: he has given himself an isolated Queen's Pawn. The chief characteristic of an isolated Pawn is that it must be guarded by *pieces*: thus, White will *attack*, Black will *defend*; White will have a lasting initiative, Black will be permanently passive. Note that the isolated Pawn cannot advance, so that Black has no way of ridding himself of this millstone.

But White has two other advantages: (1) the square Q4 *is not commanded by hostile Pawns*, and therefore it qualifies as an excellent outpost and pivot point. Black has no similarly secure post for his own minor pieces. (2) Black is weak on certain black squares (at this stage, on K4, Q3 and KB3) due to having four Pawns on white squares. It is therefore vital for Black to keep his King's Bishop on KKt2 to guard the black squares.

15 QR–B1   B–KB1?

Poor play; see the previous explanation.

16 Kt–Q4   Q–K4
17 P–QKt4   Kt–K3
18 Kt–B3   Q–Kt1
19 Q–Kt3   P–QR3

Sooner or later he must play this move to keep White's pieces out of QKt4. But now another Pawn is on white squares, weakening the black squares still more!

20 Kt–QR4   Q–Q3
21 P–QR3   P–QKt4

The defender loses patience! One can appreciate Black's desperation at having his Queen condemned to guard a mere Pawn! But now *all* the Black Pawns are on white squares, and White's pieces gain a beautiful outpost at QB5—a newly-weakened black square.

22 Kt–B5   Q–Kt3
23 Kt × Kt!

A very surprising move. Most players would have left the Knight at QB5, where he is strongly posted. Others would have played Kt × B, to get the two-Bishop advantage. The text is primarily a positional trap, into which Black falls.

23 ....   P × Kt

Relatively best was 23 ... Q × Kt, although White would still be left with a lasting initiative. The text is very natural, as it rids Black of the burdensome isolated Pawn. *But his black squares are still weak*; above all, White has control of the vital square K5.

24 B–B3!	Kt–K5
25 B–RI!	

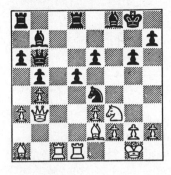

26 Q–Kt2 is threatened. A hot fight is going on for control of the long diagonal; if 26 ... B–Kt2; 27 B × B, K × B; 28 Q–Kt2*ch* with decisive advantage.

25	R–Q2
26 Kt–K5	R–QB2
27 B–Q4	Q–Q3
28 P–B3	R × R

Or 28 ... Kt–Kt4; 29 Kt–Kt4, B–Kt2; 30 B × B followed by 31 Q–Kt2! with an iron grip on the diagonal.

29 R × R	Kt–Q7
30 Q–B3	Kt–B5

31 B × Kt	KtP × B

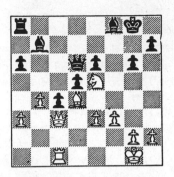

32 Kt–Kt4!	K–B2

If 32 ... P–KR4; 33 Q–B2!, K–R2; 34 Kt–K5 etc.

33 B–B5!	Q–QI
34 Q–R8!	B–Kt2
35 Q × P	Q–Kt4

On 35 ... Q–RI; 36 Kt–K5*ch* is deadly.

36 B–Q4	R–KKtI
37 P–KR4	Q–QI

Or 37 ... Q–R4; 38 Kt–K5*ch* winning at once.

38 Kt–R6*ch*	*Resigns*

Black succumbed to his weakness on the black squares.

Exploiting a Cramped Position

Unless they contain some genuine potential of counter-attacking possibilities, constricted positions are doomed to defeat or, at best, cumbersomely passive defense.

To take advantage of the disabilities which inhere in such positions, we *concentrate on their weak points*. We spy out a point or line of invasion, and thus break into the enemy's position. Sometimes there is a definite weakness on which we can concentrate, utilizing our superior freedom of movement. Sometimes mere mobility can be cumulatively increased until it results in a progressive paralysis of the opponent's position.

The important thing is to have a plan; and to have a plan, we need to understand our position and that of our opponent: to know *what to attack, and what means to use to attack it*. You will find it a useful practice to pause at about the tenth move to appraise the position, and try to foresee the prospects which are available to each player. Not to follow such a custom exposes you to the danger of being carried away by unrealistic projects, or of overlooking future weaknesses in your own game.

KING'S INDIAN DEFENSE

Hastings, 1936–37

WHITE	BLACK
W.	*G.*
Winter	*Koltanowski*
1 P–Q4	Kt–KB3
2 P–QB4	P–KKt3
3 Kt–QB3	B–Kt2
4 P–K4	P–Q3
5 P–KKt3	O–O
6 B–Kt2	P–B3
7 KKt–K2	P–K4
8 P–KR3	B–K3?
9 P–Q5	P×P
10 BP×P	B–Q2
11 O–O	Kt–K1
12 B–K3	P–Kt3?
13 P–B4	P–B3?

You note at a glance that the position of the Black King's Bishop (hemmed in by its own Pawns on black squares) is hopeless. How did this come about?

We observe that Black lost time with his unfortunate moves with the Queen's Bishop. Further,

he missed a chance to open up the position somewhat with 12 ... P–B4. True, in that event White would have replied 13 P–B4 or 13 P–B3 with a fine game, but Black would have had a much freer game than after the text.

On move 13, ... P–B4 was absolutely imperative, even though White would have obtained a clear positional advantage by 14 KP × P, KtP × P; 15 P × P, B × P; when White gets magnificent squares for his Knights at Q4 and KB4. Despite this difficulty, Black would have had more freedom and more maneuvering space, and hence more fighting chances, than he gets in the actual game.

14 P–B5!

Nailing down the King's Bishop Pawn so that ... P–B4 is permanently impossible and the King's Bishop is hemmed in for good.

14 ....   P–KKt4?

A serious positional error. He barricades the position in the hope that his King's Bishop's lack of mobility will not matter in a position where there is no entry for either side. This speculation proves futile: White can break through by advancing his King's Rook Pawn!

What were the alternatives? 14 ... P × P? is also bad: 15 P × P followed by Kt–K4, P–KKt4 and P–KR4 and Black's badly cramped position has no future.

Relatively best was an avoidance of Pawn moves. White would eventually try a Pawn storm with P–KKt4 and P–KR4. But with the Pawn position still in a fluid state, Black would have had somewhat better defensive chances than after the text.

15 P–KKt4   R–B2
16 Kt–Kt3   B–KB1
17 R–B2   Kt–Kt2

Both sides make their preparations for the coming P–KR4. But while White's maneuvers are *aggressive*, Black's are *defensive*.

It is very questionable whether Black can set up a satisfactory defensive formation.

18 B–KB1!	B–K1
19 R–R2	P–QR4
20 P–KR4!	

Beginning the final phase. If now 20 ... P × P; 21 R × P and White triples his heavy pieces on the King's Rook file against Black's Pawn.

20	P–R3
21 P × P	RP × P
22 Q–B3!	R–Kt2

Anticipating White's next move, he creates a flight square for the King.

23 Q–R1!

| 23 .... | Kt–Q2 |

He cannot disentangle his pieces. If 23 ... K–B2; 24 R–R7, K–K2; 25 Q–R6 and wins.

| 24 R–R8ch | K–B2 |
| 25 Q–R7 | K–K2 |

There was no defense to the threat of 26 Kt–R5.

26 Kt–R5   *Resigns*

For after 26 ... B × Kt; 27 P × B he has no defense whatever against the threatened P–R6. A drastic example of the evil effects of a cramped position.

The Play against Weak Color Complexes

As in the previous game, we deal here with the problem of playing against a Bishop which has little mobility because it is hemmed in by its own Pawns. Such positions arise through carelessness or lack of foresight in the opening. The damage can be done in one or two moves, and a positionally compromised game is the consequence. You will ask: "How can I tell in the opening that a Bishop is going to have little mobility during the rest of the game?"

There is an infallible indicator for this purpose: the Pawn position. In the diagram on this page, the mobility of Black's Bishop is hampered by his own Pawns on KKt4, KB5 and Q3. *This is a condition which will not be altered for the remainder of the game.*

But this is not the whole story: the Black Pawns on black squares in turn command only black squares. Certain white squares are therefore at the opponent's mercy. One of these squares (Black's KB4) is of crucial importance, and it has been *permanently* ceded to White! Maroczy's flawless play fully exploits these conditions.

RUY LOPEZ	
New York, 1924	
WHITE	BLACK
G. Maroczy	*F. D. Yates*
1 P–K4	P–K4
2 Kt–KB3	Kt–QB3
3 B–Kt5	P–QR3
4 B–R4	Kt–B3
5 O–O	B–K2
6 R–K1	P–QKt4
7 B–Kt3	P–Q3
8 P–B3	O–O
9 P–Q3	B–K3
10 QKt–Q2	Kt–KR4
11 P–Q4*!*	B × B
12 P × B	Kt–B5*?*
13 Kt–B1	Q–B1

Relatively better, despite the

loss of time involved, was ... Kt–Kt3 here or next move.

14 Kt–Kt3	P–Kt3
15 P–Q5*!!*	Kt–Q1
16 B × Kt*!*	P × B
17 Kt–K2	P–Kt4

Forced.

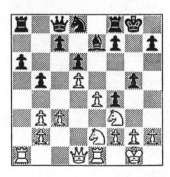

One glance at the diagram

explains why White played 16 B × Kt!. The exchange followed by 17 Kt–K2 has made ... P–Kt4 necessary, and now Maroczy is ready to play for the occupation of KB5. This, by the way, gives us his reason for 15 P–Q5!!, an interpolation which created Q4 as a pivot point on the road to KB5.

Black's Pawn position has still another unfavorable quality: *White can utilize it to open the King's Rook file.* After his forces have been disposed for maximum efficiency, his use of the open file will be decisive in short order.

18 Kt(3)–Q4   R–K1
19 Kt–B5   B–B1
20 Kt(2)–Q4

Note the value of the pivot point Q4. White's immediate threat is 21 Q–R5 winning a Pawn.

20 ....   P–KB3
21 P–Kt3!

Black must now exchange, allowing his opponent to occupy the King's Rook file with devastating effect.

21 ....   P × P
22 RP × P   P–B4

In order to be able to defend his King's Rook Pawn along the second rank, he has to create a new weakness.

23 Kt–B3   Kt–B2
24 Kt–R2!   R–R2
25 Q–R5   B–Kt2

A miserable specimen of a Bishop!

26 Kt–Kt4   Q–Q2
27 K–Kt2

White's game plays itself. He threatens to win a Pawn with 28 R–R1.

27 ....   Kt–K4
28 Kt × P!   R–Q1

Black has lost the Pawn in a different way. His collapse is only a matter of time now.

29 Kt × Kt   P × Kt

... Q × Kt loses the exchange (30 Kt–B6).

30 Kt–B5   B–B3

The Bishop is still limited to menial defensive tasks.

31 R–R1   R–KB1

32 Q–Kt4!

Cleverly gaining time to double Rooks on the King's Rook file. The threat is 33 R × QRP!, R × R?; 34 Kt–R6ch.

32 ....   K–R1
33 R–R6   P–R4

34 Kt–K3!   Q–K1

If 34 ... Q × Q; 35 Kt × Q, B–Kt2; 36 R–K6 a second Pawn falls, leaving Black in a hopeless position.

35 QR–R1   R(1)–B2
36 Q–B5   Q–KB1

If 36 ... B–Q1; 37 R–K6 is crushing.

37 Kt–Kt4

The wretched Bishop is still being hounded!

37 ....   B–Q1

White announced mate in three: 38 R × Pch, K–Kt1; 39 Q–Kt6ch and 40 R–R8 mate. A highly impressive example of how to exploit a positional advantage.

CHAPTER III

Problems of the Middle Game: The Fine Art of Tactical Play

In this section you expect to see brilliant sacrifices, and you will not be disappointed. Yet the emphasis continues to be on the center, and how it governs the course of the middle game. In each case, a successful attack is based on control of the center squares.

It is important to remember that attack is not merely a matter of inspiration: it is dependent, just as surely as the more prosaic strategical play, on the nature of the position—on a cold-blooded analysis of your opponent's resources and weaknesses.

The chapter concludes with a useful review of some of the chief tactical devices, which have innumerable applications in actual play.

The Attack against an Exposed King

Pillsbury was above all a genius of attacking play, and to such a master the assault on an exposed enemy King is always an inviting task. The exposed King who cannot castle is an easy target, so that success is generally assured.

The real interest lies in the manner of execution: will it be elegant, economical and bubbling over with surprising ideas? If the crucial question is applied to a Pillsbury game, we know that the answer will be a rousing affirmative!

*QUEEN'S GAMBIT
DECLINED*

Hannover, 1902

WHITE	BLACK
H. N.	*R.*
Pillsbury	*Swiderski*
1 P–Q4	P–Q4
2 P–QB4	P–K3
3 Kt–QB3	P–QKt3?
4 Kt–B3	B–Kt2
5 P×P	P×P
6 P–K4!	P×P
7 Kt–K5	B–Q3
8 Q–Kt4!	K–B1

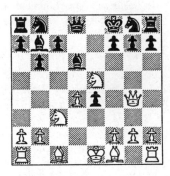

Black's fianchetto was premature; Pillsbury has reacted vigorously with a speculative Pawn sacrifice. On his eighth move Black elected to renounce castling, rather than weaken his King-side with 8 ... P–Kt3.

9 B–QB4!   B×Kt

9 ... Kt–KB3 can be answered by 10 Kt×BP with a good game for White. 10 Q–R4 is also quite strong.

10 P×B   Q–Q5

Seemingly powerful, but . . .

11 B–Q5!!

A typical Pillsbury surprise: if 11 ... B×B; 12 Q–B8*ch*, K–K2; 13 B–Kt5*ch*, P–B3; 14 R–Q1 and wins. We shall see one variation after another on this basic theme: *the insecurity of Black's King.*

11	P–QB3
12 B×KP	Q×P
13 B–B4	Kt–B3

Trying to catch up in development.

14 Q–R4!   Q–K2

If 14 ... Q–K3; 15 O–O–O! Kt–R3 (not 14 ... Kt×B?

15 R–Q8ch etc.); 16 KR–K1, Q–Kt5; 17 B–Q6ch, K–Kt1; 18 Q×Q, Kt×Q; 19 B–B3, Kt–B3; 20 R–K7 winning easily. White always "gets thar fustest with the mostest."

15 O–O–O!   Kt–K1

White was of course threatening 16 B–Q6 winning the Queen. If 15 ... Kt×B?; 16 R–Q8ch does the trick.

Black's last move drives the Queen from her powerful post at KR4, but she goes to an equally good one—and with gain of time!

**16 Q–Kt3!   Kt–R3
17 KR–K1**

Adding an important resource to the attack. If Black tries to meet the threatened 18 B×BP with 17 ... Q–B3? White wins by 18 B–Kt5, Q–K3; 19 B–B2, Q–B1; 20 R–Q8 etc.

17 ....   R–Q1

A trap: if 18 B×BP?, R×Rch! wins a piece!

18 B–Q5!

Again this ominous move! Pillsbury avoids the trap and prepares the final assault. If now 18 ... Q–B3?; 19 B–Kt5 wins.

18 ....   Q–B4

Hoping for counterplay. But Pillsbury has a crushing reply.

19 R×Ktch!   K×R

Beginning a wearisome trek, but if 19 ... R×R; 20 B–Q6ch wins the Queen!

20 Q×P   P×B

A bitter choice; if instead 20 ... R–KB1; 21 R–K1ch, K–Q2; 22 B–K6ch, K–K1; 23 B–B5ch, Q–K2; 24 R×Qch, K×R; 25 Q–K5 mate.

21 Q×Rch   K–Q2

If 21 ... K–K2; 22 B–Kt5ch wins.

22 Q×P   K–B1

Or 22 ... Q×P; 23 Q–B5ch, K–K1; 24 Q–K5ch, K–B1; 25 B–R6ch and mate next move.

23 Q×P!   P–Q5

A last attempt, for which

Pillsbury has provided with the following sardonic zigzag maneuver.

| 24 | Q-K6*ch* | R-Q2 |
| 25 | Q-Kt8*ch* | R-Q1 |

| 26 | Q-Kt4*ch* | R-Q2 |
| 27 | B-K3*!* | |

Ingenious: a pin is defeated by a counterpin.

| 27 | .... | B×P |

... K-B2 was a bit better—not enough to matter.

| 28 | R×P | *Resigns* |

Black must lose a piece. The freshness and vigor of Pillsbury's attacking play were heartwarming. This delightful game is a convincing example of what happens to an inadequately shielded King.

Crushing King-side Attack Resulting from Monopoly of the Center; Utility of a Pivot Point

When a player exchanges one of his center Pawns (King's Pawn or Queen's Pawn) for an enemy Bishop's Pawn, he is "giving up the center." Unless he is careful, his opponent may be able to monopolize the center by placing Pawns on K4 and Q4.

After the Pawns have reached K4 and Q4, there is a considerable possibility of the King's Pawn advancing to K5, as in the diagram on the following page. Whenever this happens, there is a strong likelihood of King-side attack for two reasons:

(1) With the Pawn at K5, the defender is unable to keep a Knight at his KB3—the best defense for the castled position, as it guards the vulnerable point KR2 and keeps the attacking party's Queen away from KKt4 and KR5. If KB3 is not available to the Knight, a host of sacrificial combinations becomes possible.

(2) The advance of the Pawn to K5 clears the square K4 as a kind of depot for the arrival and departure of attacking forces. In the following game, this important "pivot point" is used by three White pieces as they advance to the attack!

QUEEN'S GAMBIT

St. Petersburg, 1909

WHITE	BLACK
L. Forgacs	E. Cohn
1 P–Q4	P–Q4
2 Kt–KB3	P–K3
3 P–B4	Kt–KB3
4 Kt–B3	P×P
5 B–Kt5	B–K2
6 P–K4	P–KR3?
7 B×Kt!	B×B
8 B×P	Kt–Q2
9 O–O	O–O
10 P–K5	B–K2

Black has played the opening very poorly: he has neglected the liberating ... P–QB4 *and thus allowed the building up of a powerful White Pawn center.* Nor is this all: the prospects for Black's further development are bad, and he has seriously weakened his castled position with ... P–KR3? Bearing in mind the fact that his Knight cannot stand guard at KB3, we can conclude that Black's disabilities must cost him the game.

11 Q–K2

In order to play Q–K4 followed by B–Q3, which will threaten mate and force the new weakness ... P–KKt3. Another object of the text is to make room for a White Rook at Q1, threatening P–Q5 with unbearable pressure on the Queen's file.

11 ....   R–K1

Intending to answer Q–K4 and B–Q3 with ... Kt–B1, thus avoiding the weakening ... P–KKt3. But White has other ways of increasing his advantage.

12 QR–Q1!   P–QB3

He cannot permit P–Q5 and the resulting opening of the

Queen's file. But the text will block the action of Black's QB when it reaches QKt2.

13 Q–K4

The Queen makes use of the pivot point K4 to reach the King-side.

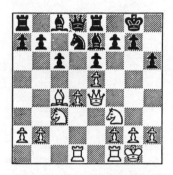

13	....	Q–B2
14	KR–KI	Kt–BI
15	Q–Kt4	P–QKt3
16	Q–R5	B–Kt2

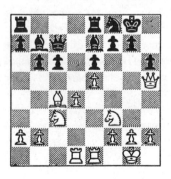

White's pieces are all *aggressively* posted, whereas Black's are miserably confined to the last two ranks. Now White again makes use of the pivot point K4.

17 R–K4!   B–Kt5

Clearing the second rank for defensive purposes; if instead 17 ... P–QB4; 18 R–B4, B–QI; 19 P–Q5 and the pressure becomes crushing, for example 19 ... P×P; 20 Kt×P, B×Kt; 21 B×B and Black can resign.

18	R–Kt4	B×Kt
19	P×B	

Having a certain and quick win, White does not concern himself with the sacrificial possibility 19 Q×P, Kt–Kt3; 20 Q–R5, B×KtP; 21 Kt–Kt5 etc. —which should also win.

19	....	K–RI
20	Kt–Kt5	R–K2
21	Kt–K4	

Again he uses the pivot point!

21	....	R–QI
22	R–Q3!	

Now this Rook joins the attack. Black's days are numbered

22	....	P–QB4

Much, much too late.

23 Kt–B6!

Threatens 24 Q × P*ch!*, P × Q; 25 R–Kt8 *mate*—a graphic illustration of White's thorough command of the board.

23	Kt–Kt3
24 R–R3	*Resigns*

Black is absolutely helpless against the coming 25 Q–Kt5 and 26 R × P*ch!*

The whole game is a perfect example of the advantages which accrue to the attacker after he advances his Pawn to K5. Note also the exploitation of the weakening ... P–KR3?.

The Attack on an Open File

Chess is a dynamic game: until you have forced checkmate or your opponent has resigned, you are confronted with one problem after another. Suppose, for example, you play to obtain a certain kind of advantage. You are successful: what then? Your work begins anew—how are you going to exploit the newly achieved advantage?

In this game White plays to obtain a broad center. He obtains it. What has he accomplished? *For the center must be turned to advantage.* But how? The solution is fascinating: White deliberately breaks up the center in order to open up the King's Bishop file as a line of attack. In other words, White *sacrifices* the beautiful center in order to create an even more powerful instrument of attack.

Thus the game preaches a powerful moral: the Pawn center is not an end in itself in this case. The Pawn center is useful only in the degree that it can lead to another, more conclusive, advantage.

QUEEN'S INDIAN DEFENSE

Western Championship, 1932

WHITE	BLACK
F. Reinfeld	S. Reshevsky
1 P-Q4	Kt-KB3
2 P-QB4	P-K3
3 Kt-KB3	P-QKt3
4 P-KKt3	B-Kt2
5 B-Kt2	P-B4?
6 P-Q5!	P×P
7 Kt-R4	P-Kt3
8 Kt-QB3	P-KR3
9 O-O	P-R3
10 P×P	P-Q3
11 P-K4	B-Kt2
12 P-B4	

Black has played the opening badly (5 ... B-K2 is much better than 5 ... P-B4?).

White has built up a broad center which is immune from attack. He has plenty of terrain on which to develop his pieces favorably, and the eventual threat of P-K5 hangs over Black's head like a veritable sword of Damocles.

Black has no firm foothold in the center. His position is cramped, his pieces have little mobility, and his chances of posting his Rooks favorably are just about nil.

12 .... KKt-Q2

Preventive measure against the possibility of P-K5. But in any event, White is in no hurry about this advance. He remembers Tarrasch's vital maxim: *when you intend to make a basic alteration in the position, do not do so until you have posted all your forces with maximum efficiency!*

13 P-R4

Preventing Black from getting any counterplay on the Queen's wing with ... P-QKt4.

13 .... O-O
14 B-K3 K-R2

He tries to protect his weakened King-side Pawn formation.

15 Q-B2!

In order to swing the Queen's Rook into action, and also with a view to commencing operations on the diagonal (White's Queen and Black's King are on the same line!).

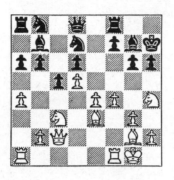

15 ....   Kt–KB3
16 P–KR3

Partly to prevent a possible ... Kt–Kt5, partly to prepare for P–KKt4 if that advance proves necessary.

16 ....   QKt–Q2
17 QR–K1   R–K1

Still trying to restrain the inevitable P–K5.

18 B–B2

At this point White's intention is P–KKt4 followed by B–Kt3 and eventually P–K5.

18 ....   Kt–KKt1

Seeing through his opponent's plan, Black musters still more

force against the coming P–K5. But the text gives White the idea for a novel attack.

19 P–K5!!

Apparently giving away the priceless Pawn on a silver salver. What can White be getting at?!

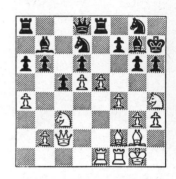

19 ....   P×P
20 P–B5!!

The point: if 20 ... P–KKt4?; 21 P–B6ch, K–R1; 22 P × Bch winning a piece. Or if 21 ... P–K5; 22 Kt×P threatening 23 Kt×Pch and mate next move.

Consequently the opening of the King's Bishop file is forced.

20 ....   Kt–B1

If 20 ... P×P; 21 Kt×P with the decisive threat of 22 Kt–Q6ch.

21 P×Pch   P×P

| 22 B–K4 | Q–Q3 |
| 23 B–K3 | Kt–K2 |

Black had to be on his guard against 24 R × Kt!.

| 24 R–B7 | K–Kt1 |
| 25 QR–KB1 | |

The tie-up of Black's forces is really fearful: if 25 ... Kt–B4; 26 R × B, Kt × B; 27 Q–B2! (threatening 28 Q–B7ch and 29 Q × B *mate*), Kt–B4; 28 B × Kt, P × B; 29 R × Bch etc.

| 25 .... | Kt × P |

No balm in Gilead.

26 R × B!

The simplest.

| 26 .... | Kt × B |
| 27 Q–B2! | |

Again threatening mate in two by Q–B7ch etc.

| 27 .... | Kt–B4 |
| 28 Kt × Kt | |

Or 28 B × Kt and Black must lose a piece, for if 28 ... P × B; 29 R × Bch!

| 28 .... | P × Kt |
| 29 Q × KBP | K–R1 |

Mate in two was again threatened!

30 R–KB7!?

Threatening 31 R × Ktch and 32 Q–R7 *mate*. White "had" to move quickly because his opponent was terribly pressed for time, else he would have played 30 Q–B7, Kt–K3; 31 Q–Kt6, Q–Q5ch; 32 K–R1, Kt–B1; 33 Q × B mate.

| 30 .... | Kt–Kt3 |

Black overstepped the time limit (40 moves in two hours), but his game would have been quite hopeless after the loss of a piece by 31 Q × Kt.

The Attack against a Weakened King-side

To combine a cramped development with organic weaknesses is to court disaster in modern chess. Black's development in the following game is so faulty that after ten moves or so, his coming defeat is clearly foreshadowed. When Black adds an irrational Pawn advance on the King-side, he exposes himself to a series of brilliant and drastic sacrifices. Black's King is massacred in splendid isolation, with none of his pieces on hand for defensive purposes.

Although White's lively play makes a delightful impression, we must bear in mind that *every sacrifice has been made possible by Black's foolish policy of weakening the King's position.*

KING'S FIANCHETTO DEFENSE

Meran, 1926

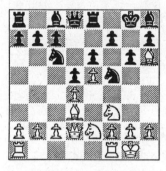

WHITE	BLACK
D. Przepiorka	J. Patay
1 P–K4	P–KKt3
2 P–Q4	P–Q3
3 Kt–KB3	B–Kt2
4 B–Q3	P–K3?
5 O–O	Kt–K2?
6 B–K3	O–O
7 Q–Q2	R–K1
8 B–KR6	B–R1
9 Kt–B3	QKt–B3
10 Kt–K2	P–Q4?
11 P–K5	Kt–B4

Black's position is very bad. His pieces have little scope: his Queen's Bishop can never come into action, and his Queen's Rook is similarly in exile. His ill-judged 4 ... P–K3? and 10 ... P–Q4? are out of keeping with the fianchetto; should the King's Bishop disappear, the black squares on the King-side will be very weak and easily accessible to invasion.

At move 10, Black should have tried ... P–K4 with a game of

sorts. As matters stand, White's Pawn at K5 is a formidable wedge which, as we know, may become the basis of a crushing attack.

12 B–KB4   P–B3
13 P–B3   P–KKt4??

Suicide. 13 ... P × P was relatively best.

14 Kt × KtP!

The beginning of a deep combination.

14 ....   P × Kt
15 B × P   Q–Q2

There is nothing really good; thus if 15 ... Kt(4)–K2; 16 Q–B2 or 15 ... Kt(3)–K2; 16 P–KKt4, Kt–Kt2; 17 Q–B2 —in either event with a winning game for White.

16 P–KKt4!   P–KR3

He does not care for 16 ... Kt–Kt2; 17 Q–B2, which leaves White with a comfortably winning position.

17 P × Kt   P × B

Reckoning on 18 Q × Pch?, Q–Kt2 and the attack is over. But of course Przepiorka has better uses for the newly opened King's Knight file!

18 P–B6!

White's powerful King's Pawn

is joined by an even mightier comrade.

18 ....   K–B2

This looks like a good defensive try (if 19 Q × P??, R–KKt1 wins White's Queen).

19 B–Kt6ch!!

With this very fine and unexpected sacrifice, the combination really begins to hit hard at Black's toppling King-side.

19 ....   K × B

Why not? If 19 ... K–B1; 20 B × R or 20 Q × P wins easily.

20 Q–Q3ch!

20 Q–B2ch? would be a mistake, as the Queen is headed for the King-side.

20 ....   K–R3

If 20 ... K–B2; 21 Q–R7ch and *mate* in two more moves.

21 Q–R3*ch*　　　K–Kt3

Doubtless hoping for the pedestrian 22 Kt–Kt3, to which 22 ... Q–R2 is an adequate reply.

22 Kt–B4*ch!!*

Another inspired sacrifice. White has his eye on the King's Knight file.

22 ....　　　　P×Kt

23 K–R1*!*

This *quiet* move almost shocks us after the previous violence! The idea is to attack Black's King on the open file. Black's situation is such (as a consequence of his bad opening play) that he is helpless against the further unfolding of the attack.

23 ....　　　　B×P

Black's last hope. 23 ... Q–R2 leads to mate in three moves.

24 R–Kt1*ch*　　　B–Kt4

25 R×B*ch!*

This ends it all. Study the above diagram and you can verify the utter bankruptcy of Black's opening play.

25 ....　　　　K×R

26 R–Kt1 *mate*

An extraordinary conclusion to an extraordinary attack.

Typical Middle Game Motifs

In the middle game there are certain types of combinations which occur again and again. Some of the most common are reviewed on the following pages:

As you study these diagrams, note which side moves first; then cover up the text below the diagram, and try to determine how you would proceed if you were playing the winning side.

White moves. He reinforces the pin on the Knight with 1 Q–B4*!.* After 1 ... Kt–K3; 2 Q–R4*ch!,* Q–B3 (forced) he pins (and wins) the Queen with 3 B–QKt5*!.*

White moves. No sign of a pin here! But after 1 P–K8(Q)*ch!,* K×Q White pins the Rook fatally with 2 B–R4. White's extra material will win easily.

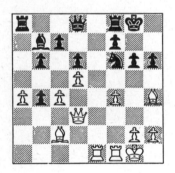 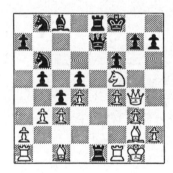

White moves. 1 R–K6*!* exploits the pin inexorably. The Knight is lost, for if 1 ... P×R; 2 Q×P*ch,* K–R1; 3 B×Kt*ch* and 4 Q–R7 *mate.*

White moves. 1 Kt×Q, R×R*ch;* 2 K×R, B×Q; 3 Kt×P is much inferior to 1 B–QR3*!!,* Q×B; 2 Q×P *mate*—or 1 ... B×Kt; 2 B×Q*ch* winning.

White moves. 1 Q×R*ch!* wins a whole Rook, for 1 ... R×Q is answered by 2 Kt-K6*ch* followed by the capture of Black's Queen. This leaves White a piece up.

White moves. He cannot play 1 Kt×P*ch* because the Knight is pinned. But after 1 Q×R*!*, BP×Q; 2 Kt-B7*ch* and 3 Kt×Q he is the exchange ahead.

Black moves. The immediate ... Kt-K7*ch* does not work. Therefore: 1 ... Q×B*!* (threatens mate); 2 P×Q, Kt-K7*ch* and Black will be a piece ahead.

Black moves. Is White's Knight securely guarded? No, for 1 ... Q×Kt*ch!*; 2 Q×Q, Kt-K6*ch* followed by 3 ... Kt×Q leaves Black a piece ahead.

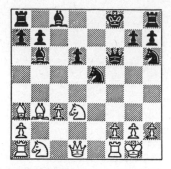 

White moves. He wins at least a piece with 1 Kt×Kt, for if 1 ... Q×Kt; 2 B×P*ch* wins the Queen. The line-up from QR3 to KB8 is a provocation.

White moves. By interpolating 1 B×Kt, B×B White is able to win a Rook with 2 Q–K4 (note the mate threat). Black can stop the mate, but his Rook goes lost.

 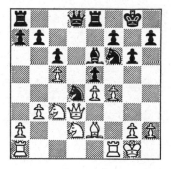

Black moves. The apparent security of White's game is brutally shattered with 1 ... R×B*!*. After 2 R×R Black plays 2 ... B×P*ch* and 3 ... B×R.

Black moves. He has a surprising win of a piece with 1 ... Kt×B*ch!*; 2 Q×Kt (forced; why?), Q–Q5*ch* winning the unguarded Knight at White's B3.

White moves. He wins the Black Queen with 1 **Q–K6***ch*, **K–R2** (or 1 ... **K–R4**); 2 **Kt–B6***ch*. The position of Black's King and Queen is most unfortunate.

White moves. By playing 1 **P–Q5***!*. White attacks the Queen and discovers attack on the Knight. The latter piece is lost.

Black moves. He wins the exchange with 1 ... **Kt–K6**; 2 **R–K1** (forced; why?), **Kt–B5***ch*; 3 **B×Kt, R×R**. Such "discoveries" occur frequently.

Black moves. He wins a piece with the discovered attack 1 ... **P–Q6***!* If 2 **Q×P, Q×B**. If 2 **B×Q, P×Q** and White must lose the Bishop or the Rook.

White moves. He is the exchange ahead, and after 1 R–R8*ch!*, K×R; 2 P–K6*ch*, Q–Kt2; 3 B×Q*ch*, K×B he has the decisive advantage of Queen for two minor pieces.

White moves. He wins a piece with 1 R–K7, B×Kt (what else?); 2 R×P*ch*, K–R1; 3 R×B*ch*, K–Kt1; 4 R×B. This is an example of the "windmill" process.

Black moves. He wins the exchange with 1 ... Kt×P*!*; 2 Q× Kt, Q×Q*ch*; 3 K×Q, P–B6*ch*; 4 Kt×B, P×R; 5 R×R*ch*, R×R (or even 5 ... K×R*!*).

Black moves. He seems to be on the defensive, but he makes use of a winning discovered check: 1 ... Q×R*ch!*; 2 K×Q, Kt–B4*ch* coming out a Rook ahead.

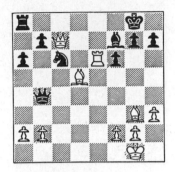

White moves. He has a win with the stunning surprise 1 R–K8*ch!* Black's overburdened Bishop cannot retake, and after 1 ... R × R; 2 Q × B*ch* White forces mate.

White moves. To remove the defender of the threatened mate at KKt7, he plays the striking 1 R–K8*!!*. Black's Queen is overburdened. He must resign.

White moves. 1 Q–K5*!!* overburdens Black's Queen beyond endurance: mate is threatened at KKt7. If 1 ... Q × Q; 2 R × R *mate.* Black's Queen is lost.

Black moves. The surprising move 1 ... Kt–B4*!!* overburdens White's Knight. If 2 Kt × Kt, R × B*ch* followed by 3 ... B × Kt wins a piece.

White moves. After 1 **Q–K6***ch*, Black protects his Knight with 1 ... **K–Kt2**. But then 2 **Q–K7***ch* (still attacking the Knight) forces the King away.

White moves. Black has no escape for his Knight. White wins a piece with 1 **B–B8***!*, **B×B** (nothing better); 2 **R×B***ch*, **K–Kt2**; 3 **K×Kt**.

Black moves. If 1 ... **Q×Q**; 2 **Kt×Q**, **B×P***ch* gaining a Pawn. But there is a better move: 1 ... **B×Kt***!* removing the protection of White's Queen.

Black moves. White's Queen must stand guard against the possibility of ... **Q–R8** *mate.* Therefore: 1 ... **R–K6***!*; 2 **Q–Kt2**, **R×P** wins.

White moves. He utilizes the seemingly doomed passed Pawn very cleverly: 1 R–Q8*ch!* (but not 1 R–B8*ch?*, K×R; 2 R–Q8*ch*, R–K1), R×R; 2 R–B8*ch*, K×R; 3 P×R(Q)*ch*.

White moves. He clears the way for the passed Pawn with 1 R×B*!*, R×R; 2 R×R, K×R (if 2 ... Q×R; 3 Q–Q8 *mate*); 3 Q–Q7*ch*, Q×Q; 4 P×Q and 5 P–Q8(Q).

White moves. An instance of "underpromotion": 1 Q×P*ch!!*, P×Q; 2 P–Kt7*ch*, K–R2; 3 P×R(Kt)*ch!*, K–R1; 4 R–Kt8 *mate!*

Black moves. Having tied up his opponent effectively, Black wins *two* pieces with 1 ... R×Kt*ch!*; 2 K×R, P–K7; 3 R–B1 (forced), P×R(Q)*ch*; 4 K×Q, Kt×B.

White moves. He has an interesting win with 1 R×P*!!*. If then 1 ... Q×Q (or 1 ... Kt×R; 2 Q–B8*ch* and mate next move); 2 R–K8 *mate!*

Black moves. White expects 1 ... R×Q*?*; 2 Kt×R*ch* and 3 Kt×Q with a win for White. But Black plays 1 ... Q×Kt*!* so that if 2 P×Q, R–Q8*ch* etc.

Black moves. 1 ... B×P*!* wins outright, for if 2 Q×B or 2 R×B, Q–B8*ch* leads to mate. Or 2 Q–Kt3, Q–B8*ch*. Successful attack on the last rank!

Black moves. He concludes superbly with 1 ... Kt–Kt5*!!* threatening 2 ... Q–R7 *mate* or 2 ... R–B8 *mate*. It is impossible for White to meet both threats.

CHAPTER IV

Problems of the Middle Game:
The Fine Art of Defensive Play

If we chessplayers had our way, we would always be attacking! The defensive, by some mystery of wishful thinking, would be banished from our play. But since we are often forced on the defensive, we owe it to ourselves to play as best we can under disagreeable conditions. "He is happy whose circumstances suit his temper," says Hume, "but he is more excellent who can suit his temper to any circumstance."

In the previous chapters, we have stressed the advantageous features of the initiative and the attack, and correspondingly emphasized the disadvantages of passive defense. Assuming, however, that we find ourselves on the defensive, we must try to make the best of the situation.

As we shall see from the following game, defensive play calls for tactical skill, foresight, resourcefulness and cool nerves. It is also one of the most useful of all the arts of chess: persevering defensive play will salvage many a hopeless-looking position.

To Attack or Not to Attack?

Some decisions can be arrived at by analyzing variations. Others—the more important decisions as to broad policy—are generally a matter of intuitive judgment, of temperament, of inclination. If our decision is not logically grounded in the realities of the position, the penalty will very likely be a serious setback. The more important the decision, the more catastrophic the consequences.

In the following example, White goes astray right in the opening: *faulty exchanges in the center* allow Black to develop at White's expense. It behooves White to realize that he has forfeited the initiative and that he must accommodate himself to the role of defender—galling as such a decision may be. Instead of reasoning in a level-headed manner about the disagreeable situation in which he finds himself, White decides to play for attack "at any cost." The cost is heavy indeed!

*QUEEN'S GAMBIT
DECLINED*

Gyor, 1930

WHITE	BLACK
B. Hoenlinger	I. Kashdan
1 P–Q4	Kt–KB3
2 P–QB4	P–K3
3 Kt–KB3	P–Q4
4 Kt–B3	P–B3
5 P–K3	QKt–Q2
6 B–Q3	P×P
7 B×BP	P–QKt4
8 B–Q3	P–QR3
9 Kt–K4	

This is altogether too tame. 9 P–K4, P–B4; 10 P–K5 leads to the most complicated and most promising possibilities in this (Meran) variation.

| 9 .... | P–B4! |

The characteristic freeing move in this opening.

| 10 P×P? | |

This exchange, which practically forces the following one, permits Black to develop at White's expense; a perfect example of a faulty exchange of center Pawns.

10	Kt×P
11 Kt×Kt	B×Kt
12 O–O	B–Kt2

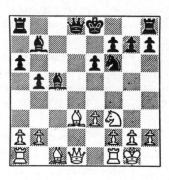

Study this position, and you will see that Black is actually ahead in development! He has brought out all three minor pieces, while White's Queen's

Bishop is still at home. True, White has already castled; but it will take two moves to develop the Queen's Bishop, thus presenting Black with a tempo that can be put to good advantage.

Where did Black obtain his lead in development? It arose from White's 9th, 10th and 11th moves, whereby he moved his Queen's Knight twice, only to exchange it and develop Black's unmoved King's Bishop at the same time. Recognizing this state of affairs, White should admit his mistake and decide that all he can reasonably expect is equality.

If White reasons along these lines, he might well conclude that playing for a symmetrical position is his best chance. In that event he might continue with 13 P–QR3, O–O; 14 P–QKt4, B–Q3; 15 B–Kt2, Q–K2. The position would then be symmetrical—but with Black a move ahead! But that need not be fatal, since in that case White would be no worse off than Black normally is in the opening and early middle game.

But White's thoughts take a wholly different turn. Realizing that his treatment of the opening has been inferior, he determines to make amends. He will play for the initiative, which "right-

fully" belongs to him because he has the White pieces. And the logical requirement for this is *to avoid symmetry!* Hence White's following moves.

13 P–QKt3   O–O
14 B–Kt2   Q–K2

Black has an easy game, for his pieces are effectively posted, and ... B–R6 is now a threat. If the Bishops are exchanged, the black squares on the Queen-side will become woefully weak (see Black's 19th and 20th moves).*

15 R–B1

Stubbornly continuing with his plan. He could have avoided ... B–R6 by playing 15 P–QR3, but this would have entailed one of these two annoying consequences:

* For extensive treatment of the subject of weak squares, see pp. 36 and 40.

(1) Either White would play P–QKt4 in order to remove the threat against his Queen's Rook Pawn, making R–B1 possible—in which case White would be two tempi behind, with just the symmetrical position he despises.

(2) Or White would have to keep his Queen's Rook at R1 in order to guard the Queen's Rook Pawn. But in that event White's Queen's Rook would be immobilized indefinitely, and Black would gain further ground by having both Rooks in play, while one of White's Rooks would be paralyzed.

15 ....   QR–B1

If 15 ... B–R6; 16 B × B, Q × B; 17 R–B7 is annoying.

16 Q–K2   B–R6
17 KR–Q1   Kt–Q4!

Observe how "one thing leads to another." White's adoption of an illogical plan resulted in a weakening of the black squares, which in turn permits the Black Knight to become powerfully entrenched at QB6.

18 B–Kt1

Nevertheless, White continues with his plan, which, as will be seen, has some dangerous implications for Black's King.

18 ....   B × B

19 Q × B   P–Kt5

Consistently working on the black squares. The Knight is now ready to go to QB6.

20 Q–K5

Necessary, else the Queen will be completely shut out by ... Kt–B6.

20 ....   Kt–B6

Not only attacking the King's Rook, but also menacing ... Kt–K7ch.

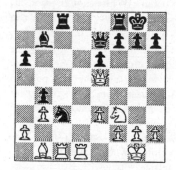

White must react energetically, but how? Obviously, by seeking some advantage on Black's apparently unguarded King-side.

But here Kashdan reveals his true stature as a master. *His plan provided not only for play on the Queen-side but for adequate defense on the other wing as well.* Thus, if now 21 B × Pch?!, K × B; 22 Q–R5ch, K–Kt1;

23 Kt–Kt5, B–K5!; 24 R×Kt, B–Kt3! and wins. So Hoenlinger tries a different tack.

21 R×Kt

Under the impression that he is eliminating the ... B–K5 defense.

21 ....   P×R!

The right way to recapture. The powerful passed Pawn is Black's ace in the hole.

22 B×P*ch*   K×B
23 Q–R5*ch*   K–Kt1
24 Kt–Kt5

Obviously 24 ... B–K5 would now be pointless—has White's illogical scheme triumphed after all?!

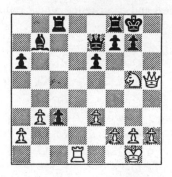

24 ....   B–K5!!

Bravo—this move is not point-

less, as Black gains a precious tempo for beating back White's offensive.

25 Kt×B   P–B7
26 R–QB1

A last desperate trap: the apparently murderous 26 ... Q–R6? is answered by 27 Kt–B6*ch!*, P×Kt; 28 Q–Kt4*ch* etc. with a draw by perpetual check!

26 ....   KR–Q1!
27 P–KR3

Or 27 P–KR4, Q–R6; 28 Kt–Kt5, Q×R*ch*; 29 K–R2, R–B2 and White has nothing but two harmless checks.

27 ....   P–B4

27 ... Q–R6 also works.

28 Kt–Kt5   Q×Kt!

Neat play.

29 Q×Q   R–Q8*ch*
30 K–R2   R×R
    Resigns

This charming game is highly instructive because it shows how a lackadaisical treatment of the opening, a though not fatal in itself, may lead to a faulty estimate of the ensuing position, with ultimate disaster as the logical outcome. *Chagrin is a poor basis for planning!*

Defense to a Direct King-side Attack

Defensive play calls for unremitting skill, application, perseverance and *faith*. No man ever had greater faith in the validity of defense than did Wilhelm Steinitz. It was his belief that any position, no matter how cramped, which had not been weakened organically, was capable of successful defense.

By organic weakness we mean a fundamental defect, such as an irreparably bad Pawn position, the permanent impossibility of developing a piece, and the like. Most players shy away from uncomfortably constricted positions; but it was Steinitz's particular delight to hold such difficult situations intact and thereby stave off the collapse which is almost inevitable in the games of weaker players.

Holding the theories he did, Steinitz accepted all gambits, going to the most incredible lengths to retain the gambit Pawn: no inconvenience was too great, and come what might, he kept his stubborn clutches on the extra Pawn.

The following game was played in Steinitz's last tournament but one, when he was a feeble man of 62. He handles the whole encounter with a steadfastness and consistency which put many a younger player to shame.

BISHOP'S GAMBIT		4 Q–R5	Kt–Kt3
Vienna, 1898		5 Kt–QB3	Q–K2
		6 P–Q4	Kt–B3
WHITE	BLACK	7 Kt–B3	Q–Kt5
D. Janowski	*W. Steinitz*	8 Q–Q5	Kt–Q1
1 P–K4	P–K4	9 P–QR3	Q–K2
2 P–KB4	P×P	10 O–O	P–Q3

Naturally!

11 Q–KR5	P–QB3
12 B–Q2	

3 B–B4   Kt–K2

An unusual defense, played to hold the gambit Pawn.

"What is this?!" we exclaim in astonishment; does Steinitz

expect to win this game? Indeed he does! His pieces are undeveloped or else badly posted, it is not clear how he will be able to castle; but Steinitz is not dismayed. He still retains his booty, and he knows that if White hopes to succeed, *he must open up the position.*

Crafty old Steinitz knows from past experience that if he plays with determination and alertness when the position is opened up, he should be able to find better squares for his pieces. And so it turns out!

12 ....   Kt–K3

First crisis: if Black is not bothered, he will play ... B–Q2 and ... O–O–O in comparative safety.

13 QR–KI   Q–B2

He sees that he must change his plan: if 13 ... B–Q2; 14

P–Q5, Kt–B2; 15 P×P, P×P and Black's position on the Queen-side is too weakened to permit castling on that wing.

14 P–Q5   Kt–QI
15 P–K5

Resolutely playing to open up the position dynamically so that his attacking forces will be trained on the hostile King. Can Black live through all this?!

15 ....   QP×P!
16 Kt×P   B–B4*ch!*
17 K–RI   O–O

That Steinitz was able to castle at all verges on the miraculous. But his troubles are only beginning!

18 P×P

So that if 18 ... P×P; 19 Kt×Kt, P×Kt; 20 Q×B winning a piece. But the old master has a neat reply:

18	B–K6!
19 Kt–B3	B × B

If now 20 Kt × B, P × P and Black is safe—incidentally maintaining the gambit Pawn! Janowski is therefore *compelled to take risks*, which, to be sure, he does with a right good will.

20 Kt–KKt5!	P–KR3
21 Q × Kt	P × Kt
22 Kt–Q5	

Attacking the Queen and threatening mate in two!

22	Q × P!
23 Kt–K7*ch*	K–R1

Black is still alive! If 24 Kt × Q, P × Q; or 24 Q–R5*ch*, Q–R3.

24 Q × KtP?

After this Black is a piece ahead. The best chance was 24 B × P, so that if 24 ... Q × Q?; 25 Kt × Q*ch*, K–R2; 26 Kt × R*ch* or 24 ... B–B4; 25 Q × B, R × B; 26 Q–Q3, R × Kt; 27 R × R, B–R4; 28 P–QKt4, B–Kt3; 29 P–Kt5 with a won game for White.

But after 24 B × P Steinitz would have justified his faith in the defense by playing 24 ... Kt × B!; 25 Kt × Q, B × R; 26 Kt–K7!, B–Q7; 27 Q–R5*ch*, Kt–R3; 28 Kt–Kt6*ch*, K–Kt1; 29 Kt × R, K × Kt; 30 Q × P, B–B4 and Black has a very satisfactory game. This was the crucial variation of the whole encounter!

24	Q–KR3
25 Q–QB5	Kt–K3

Parrying the threatened Kt–Kt6*ch*. White must exchange.

26 B × Kt	B × B
27 R–K5	B–K6!

Suddenly it turns out that Black has the attack, with two terrific Bishops. Janowski, a much younger man, was the first to crack. Crestfallen at the failure of his attack, he faces a dreary prospect.

28 Q–Kt5   P–KKt3!
29 Q×P   K–Kt2

And now Steinitz attacks! The threat is ... Q×Pch! followed by mate.

30 Q–B3   QR–Q1
31 P–R3   Q–R5
32 Kt–B6   B–Kt5!

Decisive, for if 33 Q–K4, B×P etc.

33 Q×B   Q×Q
34 P×Q   R–R1ch
35 R–R5   P×R
        Resigns

A magnificent display of defensive skill!

The Consequences of a Bad Variation: Meeting the Crisis

There are times when even the greatest masters, through carelessness, forgetfulness, indifference, or perhaps provocation, adopt a clearly inferior opening variation. After about ten moves or so, it is obvious that they have a bad game. The ensuing play can be very dramatic, for the master gathers his wits and begins to play with all the skill for which he is famous.

It is an absorbing spectacle, and raises a tantalizing problem: can the better player with the inferior position defeat the inferior player with the better position?! The tension mounts move by move, until the crisis is reached. It is at this stage that the insight, experience and tactical virtuosity of the master make themselves felt.

In the game that follows, Flohr, who is the grandmaster suffering the agonies of this typical experience, meets and survives the crisis with exemplary firmness.

ALEKHINE'S DEFENSE

Hastings, 1935–36

WHITE	BLACK
R. P. Michell	*S. Flohr*
1 P–K4	Kt–KB3
2 P–K5	Kt–Q4
3 P–QB4	Kt–Kt3
4 P–Q4	P–Q3
5 P×P	Q×P?
6 P–B5	Q–K3ch
7 B–K2	Kt–Q4
8 Kt–KB3	

Frankly admitting that the whole line of play is bad, he voluntarily loses time in order to achieve a normal if restricted development.

9 O–O	P–K3
10 Kt–B3	B–K2
11 R–K1	O–O
12 Kt–K5	Q–Q1
13 Kt×Kt	P×Kt
14 B–Q3!	

Takes away the best square available to Black's Queen's Bishop (KB4).

Black's early development of the Queen was bad, as this piece will be an easy target for White's pieces. How should Black proceed?

8 ....   Q–Q2!?

A courageous move which only a player of Flohr's reputation could allow himself to play!

Flohr is in great difficulties: White threatens 15 Q–R5, P–KKt3 (15 ... P–KR3; 16 B×RP!); 16 Kt×KtP!, RP×Kt; 17 B×P, P×B; 18 Q×KtPch, K–R1; 19 R–K5 and wins. True, he can escape this catastrophe by answering 15 Q–R5 with 15 ... P–B4, but then he has lost control of his K4.

14	B–B3
15 B–KB4	P–KKt3
16 Q–Q2	R–K1
17 B–B2	B–K3
18 P–QKt4	Kt–Q2

Michell has played well up to this point; he has obtained a winning position.

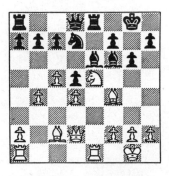

| 19 P–B6 | Kt×Kt |
| 20 P×Kt | B–K2 |

The crisis has arrived! White's proper course is now 21 P×P, R–Kt1; 22 B–R4! with a winning game.

| 21 B–R4? | P–QKt4! |

With this incisive stroke, Flohr frees himself and seizes the initiative, 22 B × P? being refuted by 22 ... R–Kt1; 23 P–QR4, P–QR3.

| 22 B–QKt3 | P–QR4! |

Another fine move, which assures Flohr of winning the Queen's Bishop Pawn and securing two connected passed Pawns.

If now 23 P–QR3, R–R3; 24 QR–B1, Q–R1!; 25 Q–B3, P–Q5!; 26 Q–Kt2, B×B; 27 Q×B, P×P; 28 P×P, R×P and wins.

23 P×P	R–R3
24 QR–B1	Q–R1
25 KR–Q1	R×RP
26 Q–K2	R–Q1
27 Q–B3	Q–B1!

Preventing 28 B×P because of the threatened 28 ... B–KKt5. Black is now ready to advance his passed Pawn.

| 28 Q–Kt3 | P–Q5! |

White's position is strategically untenable. He attempts a despairing attack which is parried with ease.

29	B–Kt5	KB×B
30	Q×B	B×B
31	P×B	R–Q4
32	R–Q3	Q–K3
33	P–B4	R–R3

If now 34 R(1)–Q1, Q×BP; 35 R×P?, Q–B4 and wins.

34	R–R3	R×BP
35	R–R1	

| 35 | .... | R–R3 |

White threatened 36 R–R8*ch*, K–Kt2; 37 Q–R6 *mate*. But Flohr calmly draws the sting from the attack and brings back the action to the center.

| 36 | R×R | Q×R |

37	Q–R6	P–Q6
38	Q×RP*ch*	K–B1
39	Q–R6*ch*	K–K2
40	Q–Kt5*ch*	K–Q2
41	Q–Kt4*ch*	Q–K3
42	Q–Q1	Q–Kt3*ch*
43	K–B1	Q–Q5*!*

Centralization!

44	Q–Q2	K–K2
45	R–B3	P–QB4
46	P–B5	R×P
47	P–B6*ch*	K–K3
48	Q–R5	

If 48 Q×P?, Q–R8*ch*; 49 K–B2, Q–K8 *mate*; or 48 R×P?, R–B4*ch*; 49 K–K1, Q–Kt8*ch*; 50 K–K2, Q–B8*ch* and mate next move.

48	....	R–B4*!*
49	Q–R6*ch*	K–K4
50	Q×P	R×R*ch*
51	P×R	K×P
52	Q–Kt6*ch*	K–Kt2
	Resigns	

A thrilling and instructive game.

Superb Defensive Play: a Peripatetic King

The dangers which confront an exposed King have been set forth endlessly in theory and practice. (We have seen a grisly example of these perils in the game Pillsbury—Swiderski, page 45.) A chess King is a delicate creature who requires solicitous protection at all times. Let him find himself in the crossfire of the enemy's pieces, and sacrifices rattle on His Majesty like hail.

Yet there is hardly a rule which does not have exceptions, and Tartakover is just the kind of iconoclast who revels in breaking precedent. "Any defense is good enough," he has written with characteristic cynicism, "if its reputation is bad enough." The way in which he light-heartedly sends his King safely to KKt6 is typical of his love for confounding the solemn authorities who rely overmuch on precept and rote. What makes his feat all the more daring is that he carries it out against one of the greatest attacking masters of all time!

From this game you can learn how to conduct a resourceful and unconventional defense, but be warned: don't go to the extreme of resorting to Tartakover's deliberately provocative tactics!

CARO-KANN DEFENSE

Copenhagen, 1923

WHITE	BLACK
R. Spielmann	S. Tartakover
1 P–K4	P–QB3
2 P–Q4	P–Q4
3 P×P	P×P
4 P–QB3	Kt–QB3
5 B–KB4	Kt–B3
6 Kt–Q2	P–KKt3

7 KKt–B3	B–Kt2
8 P–KR3	Kt–K5
9 Kt×Kt	P×Kt
10 Kt–Q2	P–B4
11 B–B4	

I. THE PROBLEM

It is Black's move, and it is time for him to take stock of the situation and make his plans for the middle game. What is the outstanding feature of the position—what is the consideration

which should influence him above everything else?

The most notable feature of the position is that Black cannot castle. The diagonal leading to his KKt1 is open, and it is not clear how Black can satisfactorily remove his disability. (We shall go into the whys and wherefores a little later.)

Another difficulty of Black's position is that after White castles and plays P–B3, the King file will be forced open with terrible pressure against the backward King's Pawn. With Black's Rooks immobilized by his inability to castle, with his King's Pawn under pressure by the hostile forces, Black would be irretrievably lost.

Can Black neutralize the pressure? Studying the diagrammed position, we conclude that the outlook is dark for Black. If 11

... P–K3, he will be able to castle, but at what a price! He will create a critical weakness at his K3, which will be subject to attack on the diagonal and on the file (after P–B3). In addition, Black's Queen's Bishop will have no scope and will be tied to the defense of the King's Pawn.

This "solution" is unsatisfactory. Since the White King's Bishop is so troublesome, perhaps Black can achieve freedom by driving the Bishop away? For example: 11 ... Kt–R4. But then there follows 12 Q–R4ch!

I. 12 ... B–Q2 (but not 12 ... Kt–B3?; 13 P–Q5); 13 B–QKt5, Kt–B3 (White threatened to win a piece with 14 B × Bch); 14 Q–Kt3, P–QR3 (if 14 ... Kt–R4; 15 B × Bch, Q × B; 16 Q–R3, Kt–B3; 17 P–B3! and Black's position is still under strong pressure); 15 B–B4, Kt–R4; 16 B–B7ch, K–B1; 17 Q–Q5 with a formidable game for White.

II. 12 ... K–B1. Black has been deprived of castling, and has a poor game.

But it is in just this kind of inordinately difficult position that Tartakover shines. Better than most players he knows that "men at some time are masters of their fate."

II. THE SOLUTION

Tartakover's solution begins with:

11 ....   P–K4!!

This move is astonishing because it opens up the game and hence apparently exposes Black's unhappy King to a devastating attack. But the important thing about the text is that it gives Black ample scope for his pieces (including the King!). The further course of the game confirms Tartakover's view that so long as his pieces are active, the King can take care of himself.

12 P×P   Kt×P

It is already a moot question whether White still has the initiative! For if 13 B–QKt3*??*, Kt–Q6*ch* wins a piece; if 13 B–Kt5*ch* Black parries comfortably with 13 ... B–Q2.

13 B×Kt

This is necessary to continue the "attack."

13 ....   B×B

Now Black can face the future with confidence. He has two Bishops, his King-side Pawns are aggressively posted and he can castle artificially with ... K–B1–Kt2.

14 Q–Kt3   Q–Kt3*!*

Tartakover's sly plan begins to unfold. He is not at all worried about the King's safety. Should the offer of the exchange of Queens be accepted, Black will stand well, because of his two Bishops, open lines, and the ease with which his King-side majority can be turned into a passed Pawn. Besides, his King would be quite safe, and Spielmann, the perennial attacker, is naturally discontented with such a picayune outcome.

15 B–Kt5*ch*   K–K2*!*
16 Kt–B4   Q–B4
17 Kt×B   Q×Kt
18 O–O–O

Spielmann has deprived his opponent of the two Bishops. The position is about even, except that White's King is quite safe, whereas the Black King seems exposed.

18 ....   B–K3

19	B–B4	B × B
20	Q × B	KR–Q1!

This move seems obvious, but it had to be calculated with some care.

| 21 | Q–Kt4*ch* | K–B3! |

Paradoxically, this advance is safer than a retreat to the first rank!

22	Q × KtP	Q–B5*ch*
23	K–Kt1	Q × P
24	Q–B6*ch*	

After 24 Q × KRP, Q × P Black's two connected passed Pawns would eventually decide in his favor.

24	....	K–Kt4!
25	P–R4*ch*	K–Kt5!!

The King moves are astonishing but highly effective. Tartakover foresees that his King will be quite safe, and the presence of

the King in the midst of White's Pawns hampers the movements of White's Rooks, which must remain on hand to guard the Pawns.

| 26 | QR–KB1 | Q–Kt3! |

This gains an important tempo. To exchange Queens would lead to a hopeless ending for White: he must retreat.

| 27 | Q–B4 | |

Threatening 28 Q–K2*ch* and mate next move.

| 27 | .... | R–Q7! |

Parrying the threat and menacing mate himself. Tartakover is a wag!

| 28 | P–Kt4 | Q–K6 |

Threatening to exchange Queens with ... Q–Q6*ch*. 28 ... R × KtP was simpler.

| 29 | R–R3 | Q–Kt3 |

30 R(3)–B3

Or 30 R–R2, QR–Q1 winning easily.

30 ....   R × KtP
31 R–B4*ch*   K–Kt6!

Curiouser and curiouser!

32 Q–Q5   R–QB1
33 Q–Q7   Q–R3
      Resigns

A very fine and original game by Tartakover. Rarely does one see an opening problem solved so ingeniously and so incisively.

CHAPTER V

All's Well that Ends Well:
How to Play Better Endings

In chess, the endgame is the "payoff." No matter how well you play, the win is not yours until you have administered checkmate or your opponent has resigned. The possibility of a last-minute blunder, undoing the effect of previous good play, is always present. As Tartakover has ironically observed, in chess "victory goes to the man who has made the next to the last blunder."

It is not surprising to learn that skilful endgame play is the hallmark of the great master. All the World Champions have been virtuosi of this department of the game. At least two (Lasker and Capablanca) have been something less than first-rate authorities on the opening; it did not matter, for in the ending they were unsurpassable.

The endgame is usually the last branch of chess to be mastered even by the immortals. At the beginning of their careers, they take the chess world by storm with their dazzling middle-game play. As they settle down, they usually devote profound study to the openings. But finished technique in the ending is the real sign of maturity.

A typical, because always recurring, situation, is described thus by Capablanca in his *Chess Fundamentals*: "Yet the ending itself was not as simple as it at first appeared, and finally —perhaps through one weak move on my part—it became a very difficult matter to find a win. Had I been a weak end-game player the game would probably have ended in a draw, and all my previous efforts would have been in vain. Unfortunately, that is very often the case among the large majority of players; they are weak in the endings; a failing from which masters of the first rank are sometimes not free."

We see, then, that it is very important to play the ending with as much exactitude and force as possible. Yet when we try to study endgame play, we run up against two difficulties. The first (let's face it!) is that the amateur generally finds the ending distasteful because it is too "simple," too lacking in those attacking possibilities which make chess so delightful. Granted that the endgame is less "glamorous" than the middle game; *the fact remains that the endgame is of enormous practical importance*, as we have seen. The second difficulty (one that cannot be blamed on the amateur) is that there is still a dearth of useful and usable books on the endgame. But this is a condition that is gradually being remedied.*

What is the endgame, and what is its chief objective? The ending is by definition the final stage of a game which has not concluded with checkmate or resignation in its earlier stages. The ending is the heir of the middle game: the players reach the ending with the assets and liabilities acquired earlier in the game. Assume that a player reaches the ending a Pawn to the good, or with the less tangible but equally positive advantage of an open file for a Rook, or command of the seventh rank, or a passed Pawn. What is that player's goal?

In almost all endgames, the objective is to queen a Pawn. With forces equal or nearly equal, that is almost the only way to wind up the game victoriously; to obtain a new Queen, securing an overwhelming advantage in material to assure

---

* If I may be excused the personal reference, I should like to call attention to my *Practical Endgame Play*, published in 1940 (London: Sir Isaac Pitman & Sons, Ltd. Philadelphia: David McKay Company). The book is divided into four parts: I. Transition to a favorable ending; II. Transition to an unfavorable ending; III. Missed opportunities; IV. Defending difficult positions.

checkmate or the opponent's resignation. Relatively few players keep this goal clearly in mind.

To study the endgame in all its forms and objectives would be a task far beyond the scope of the present book. We shall therefore confine ourselves to considering the two types of endings which occur most frequently in practical play: (1) Rook and Pawn endings, and (2) Bishop vs. Knight endings.

When you have played over and enjoyed these endings, you will realize that the colorless appearance of endgame play is quite deceptive; that there is much in it that is enjoyably intricate; that it offers exciting scope for large-scale planning; and that, above all, systematic study of the endgame will immeasurably increase your playing strength. Endings contain so many subtleties that (paraphrasing Tarrasch's famous remark about the Queen's Gambit) we might well describe them as "the chamber music of chess."

Rook and Pawn Endings

Bearing in mind that all these endgames deal with the problem of obtaining an overwhelming material superiority by queening a Pawn, we shall find the following points very useful:

MOBILITY. This is the very soul of play with the Rooks. A lack of mobility may cancel a material advantage; conversely, it may often be worthwhile to give up a Pawn in order to place a Rook on an open file, or on the seventh rank or to tie the hostile Rook down to some trifling defensive task. One of the reasons why Marshall was a superb endgame player was that his style was so aggressive.

THE PAWN POSITION. This always plays an important role in the endgame. It is here that Pawn weaknesses are seen at their worst: the attack on an isolated Pawn, on a backward Pawn, on a doubled Pawn. It is also here that the strength of useful Pawns is seen at its best: the passed Pawn, the protected passed Pawn, connected passed Pawns, the Pawn that holds back two hostile Pawns, the concentrated Pawn majority on one flank—all these bring out the *qualitative* value of Pawns.

THE KING. We are all familiar with the value of this piece in the ending. It is in this simplified stage of the game that the King can come out of hiding and be transformed into a fighting piece. Skilful maneuvering with the King is often the key to a won ending. The King escorts strong passed Pawns to the queening-square, guards his Pawns from raids by a hostile Rook, attacks the enemy's Pawns or blockades them when they have become too dangerous. Always be on the alert for favorable opportunities to *centralize* your King during the endgame.

EXCHANGING AND SIMPLIFYING. One of the pleasant features of being ahead in material is that one can often use this advantage as a weapon by threatening to simplify into an easily won King and Pawn ending—sometimes even at the cost of the extra material. Opportunities for this are more frequent than the amateur realizes; whenever available, they constitute a simple and effective method of forcing the weaker side to give way.

ZUGZWANG. There are positions where the defender is compelled, by the obligation of moving, to lose material or incur some other fatal disadvantage. This condition is known as *Zugzwang*, and when it sets in, we know that the defender's power of resistance has been broken. A good example of *Zugzwang* appears on page 98.

EXAMPLES FROM ACTUAL PLAY

EXAMPLE 1

White to move

(Monte Carlo, 1903)

MASON

SCHLECHTER

White's extra Pawn (the Queen's Bishop Pawn) is the candidate for queening. While *Black's King is cut off by White's Rook* from the main theater of action, White's King is free to aid the passed Pawn.

1 K–B2   P–R4
2 K–K1!

Not 2 K–K3? allowing the approach of Black's King (... K–K3 etc.).

2 ....   P–Kt4
3 K–Q2   K–B4
4 K–Q3   R–R1

5 P–B4   R–Q1 *ch*
6 K–B3   R–QB1

Black tries to check back White's King and at the same time to prevent the advance of the passed Pawn.

7 K–Kt4   R–Kt1 *ch*

Else P–B5 wins quickly.

8 K–R5   R–QB1
9 K–Kt5   R–Kt1 *ch*
10 K–R6   R–QB1
11 R–QB2!

Black's King can now cross, but it no longer matters.

11 ....   K–K4
12 K–Kt7   R–B4
13 K–Kt6   *Resigns*

The finish might have been: 13 ... R–B1 (not 13 ... K–Q3??; 14 R–Q3*ch*); 14 P–B5

and Black is helpless against P–B6–B7 and K–Kt7.

EXAMPLE 2
Black to move
(Carlsbad, 1907)

DUS-CHOTIMIRSKY

MIESES

Black manufactures a passed Pawn *by advancing on the wing where he has the extra Pawn.*

1	P–KKt4!
2 R–KKt1	P–Kt5
3 R–QB1	

If instead 3 P–KR3, R–Kt1 (threatens 4 ... P×P!); 4 P–KR4, P–Kt6 followed by 5 ... R–Kt5—or 4 P×P, R×P followed by the advance of Black's King; with an easy win in either case.

| 3 .... | R–Q1 |

| 4 R–B1 | R–Q6*ch* |

If now 5 K–B2, R–K6, 6 R–B5, R–K7*ch!*; 7 K–B3, R×RP; 8 R×P*ch*, K–B3; 9 R–B5*ch*, K–Kt3 and the two connected passed Pawns win very easily.

5 K–B4	R–Q5*ch*
6 K–B5	R×P
7 R–B5	P–R5
8 R–R5	P–Kt6
9 P×P	P×P
10 K–Q5	R–K7!

The hostile King is cut off from the advanced Pawn (as in the previous example); and, of course, if 11 R×P*ch*, R×R*ch*; 12 K×R, P–Kt7 and the Pawn queens.

11 R–Kt5	P–Kt7
12 P–Kt4	K–B3
13 R–Kt8	K–B4

14 R–Kt7   R–Q7*ch!*

Driving White's King still further away!

15 K–B4   K–B5
Resigns

For Black's King escorts the advanced passed Pawn to the queening-square.

EXAMPLE 3

Black to move

(Helsingfors, 1935)

FRYDMAN

STAHLBERG

Black is a Pawn ahead; his Rook can be posted aggressively; his King comes into action rapidly; and all the White Pawns, being scattered, are easily subject to attack.

1 ....   K–B2

2 P–Q5!

The most sensible course: he rids himself of a weakness, and at the same time increases his Rook's mobility. White continually threatens invasions of the seventh rank, so that the Black King must stand guard.

Passivity would be futile: 2 R–K2 (to guard against ... R–B7), R–B5; 3 R–Q2, R–R5 followed by ... K–K2–Q3–Q4 and the powerful centralization of Black's King is decisive.

2 ....   P×P
3 R×P   K–K3
4 R–Q3   R–B4

In order to keep White's Queen's Rook Pawn under observation. The amateur rarely utilizes opportunities to move his Rook effectively along a rank.

5 P–B4   R–QR4
6 P–R3   R–R5

Black's Rook has the function of attacking the Queen's Rook Pawn and the Bishop's Pawn; White's Rook has the function of guarding the Queen's Rook Pawn and also keeping Black's King out of KB4.

7 K–B3   K–B4
8 R–Q5*ch*   K–K3
9 R–Q3

Black now sees that he must change his procedure, because at present, White's Rook *has too much mobility*. Stated differently, the problem is: how can Black play in such a way that his Rook will still perform two functions, while White's Rook *will be robbed of one of its functions?*

The solution: Black will advance his Queen-side Pawns so as to obtain a passed Pawn; then he will post his Rook behind the passed Pawn, constantly threatening to advance it. This will tie up White's Rook. Observe how this logical plan works out.

9	....	R–R4
10	K–K4	P–QKt4
11	K–B3	P–R4
12	K–Kt3	P–R3
13	R–K3*ch*	K–B3
14	K–B3	R–R5
15	K–Kt3	R–B5!

| 16 | K–B3 | R–B3 |

A retreat in appearance only: he prepares to support the coming passed Pawn.

17	K–Kt3	P–R4
18	K–B3	R–Kt3
19	R–Kt3	K–B4

For the first time the King is able to occupy this all-important square — and why? — because White's Rook is already tied up by the mere threat of ... P–Kt5.

| 20 | K–K3 | P–Kt5! |

Now White must capture (21 ... P–R5! is threatened), for 21 P–QR4 is answered by ... R–QB3–B7 attacking the Queen's Rook Pawn from the rear.

| 21 | P×P | P×P |
| 22 | K–B3 | |

If instead 22 R–Kt2 or R–Kt1, R–K3*ch*; 23 K–B3, R–K5 and wins. Here we have the ideal position aimed for by Black: White's Rook performs only one function (stopping the Queen's Knight Pawn) while Black's Rook performs two functions (guarding the Queen's Knight Pawn *and* attacking the Bishop's Pawn).

| 22 | .... | P–R5! |
| | *Resigns* | |

What is White to do? If 23 K–K3, R–K3ch etc. wins. If 23 R–Kt1, P–Kt6; 24 R–Kt2, R–Kt4; 25 K–K3, R–Kt5; 26 R–Kt1, P–Kt7 and White is absolutely helpless!

A wonderfully instructive example of Rook and Pawn play.

EXAMPLE 4

White to move

(Match, 1897)

SHOWALTER

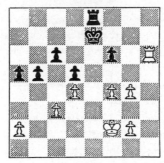

PILLSBURY

White's extra Pawn, being doubled, does not seem to count for much. Before the King's Knight Pawn can be used to advantage, *White must exploit the superior mobility of his Rook.* This is expressed in command of the seventh rank:

1 R–R7*ch*	K–Q3
2 R–KB7	K–K3
3 R–QR7	P–Kt5*!*

The best chance: if instead 3 ... P–R5; 4 P–B5*ch*, K–Q3; 5 R–KB7 wins. With the text, Black initiates a policy of counterattack—his only chance, for his Rook has no scope, and White's Rook is all-powerful.

4 R×P	P×P
5 R–B5	K–Q3
6 R×P	R–K5*!*

The point of his third move. Pillsbury now plays with masterly foresight and precision.

7 P–Kt5*!!*	P×P

If 7 ... R×P; 8 P–Kt6, R×P*ch*; 9 R–B3, R–K5 (if 9 ... R–KKt5; 10 R–KKt3 and wins, or if 9 ... R×R*ch*; 10 K×R, K–K2; 11 P–R4*!* and wins. Here, as in many other variations, the distant passed Queen's Rook Pawn decides the issue); 10 P–Kt7, R–K1; 11 R×P*ch*, K–K2; 12 R–B8*!* winning.

Or if 7 ... R×P*ch*; 8 R–B3, P×P (if 8 ... R×R*ch*; 9 K×R, P×P; 10 K–Kt4, P–B4; 11 K×P*!* and White still has time to stop Black's Pawn); 9 R×R, P×R; 10 P–R4*!*, K–B2; 11 K–B3 winning easily.

8 P×P	R×P
9 R–K3!	

Cutting off the Black King from being able to stop the Knight's Pawn. Hence Black's Rook will have to perform this function, *consequently forfeiting much of its mobility.*

9	P–B4
10 P–Kt6	R–QR5
11 P–R3	P–Q5
12 R–KKt3	R–R1
13 P–Kt7	R–KKt1
14 R–Kt5!	

White's last move has prevented Black's King from advancing. If now 14 ... K–B3; 15 P–R4!, P–B5; 16 K–K2, P–B6; 17 K–Q3, K–Kt3; 18 P–R5ch, K–R3; 19 K×P, P–B7; 20 R–QB5, R×P; 21 R×P and wins, as Black's King is cut off.

14	P–B5
15 K–K2	K–K3
16 P–R4	K–B3
17 R–Kt3	K–B4

He must not capture the Pawn!

18 P–R5	K–B5
19 R–B3ch	K–K5

If 53 ... K–Kt5; 54 R–B7 wins easily.

20 R–B7	P–Q6ch
21 K–Q2	K–Q5
22 R–Q7ch!	K–B4
23 P–R6	R–K1

A last attempt.

24 P–R7	K–Kt5
25 R–Kt7ch	K–B4
26 R–Kt8	R–K7ch
27 K–Q1	P–B6

So that if either Pawn queens, Black can win by 28 ... P–B7ch followed by 29 ... R–K8ch etc.

28 R–B8ch!	K–Q5
29 R–B4ch!	K–K6
30 P–R8(Q)	P–B7ch
31 R×P	R–K8ch
32 K×R	*Resigns*

A masterpiece of energetic and imaginative play. It is an impressive example of the importance of aggressive tactics in Rook and Pawn endings.

EXAMPLE 5

Black to move

(Vienna, 1908)

SWIDERSKI

LEONHARDT

The forces are even, but Black has *a distant passed Pawn*. At first sight, it seems that White has an excellent position because of his Rook on the seventh rank. Actually, however, he has a bad game: Black's passed Pawn is very strong, and his King is far more active than the White monarch.

1 ....   P–B5!

He loses no time in advancing the formidable Pawn.

2 K–B1   P–QKt4
3 P–Kt4

Hoping to secure a passed Pawn on the wing where he has a Pawn majority. But this will turn out to be too slow.

3 ....   K–Kt3
4 R–KB7   P–B6
5 K–K1   R–Q1!

Very important: White's King has no chance of approaching the passed Pawn, thus enabling Black to discard defensive tactics (if now 6 R × P?, P–B7 etc.).

7 R–B2   P–Kt5
8 P–KR4   R–Q5
9 R–KKt2   K–Kt4
10 P–R5   P–Kt6!

Enabling Black's King to assist in the queening process.

11 P × P   K–Kt5
12 P–Kt5   K × P
13 P–Kt6   P × P
14 R × P

Obviously, if 14 P × P, P–B7 wins at once.

14	....	P–B7
15	R–Kt6*ch*	K–R6
16	R–R6*ch*	K–Kt5

If now 17 R–R1, K–Kt6 is decisive.

| 17 | R–Kt6*ch* | K–B4 |
| | *Resigns* | |

The Pawn must queen. Very fine play by Black.

EXAMPLE 6

Black to move

(Barmen, 1905)

TCHIGORIN

MARSHALL

White labors under the fundamental inferiority of an *organically weak Pawn position* (Queen's Pawn and Queen's Rook Pawn). This difficulty might be bearable if White could obtain *aggressive*

positions for his pieces—if, for example, Black now proceeded with 1 ... R–B6*ch*; 2 K–K4, R × RP allowing 3 R–QB2, with counterchances for White. But Tchigorin chooses the safest, because simplest, way:

1	....	K–K3!
2	R–Kt3	K–Q4
3	R–Q3	P–B4

Establishing *Zugzwang*, as White must now lose a Pawn (if 4 R–Q2, R–B6*ch*; 5 R–Q3, R × R*ch*; 6 K × R, P–QR4! and Black wins easily with 7 ... P–Kt5, obtaining a distant passed Pawn).

4	P–R3	P–KR4
5	K–K2	R × P
6	R–QB3	R–K5*ch*

If now 7 K–B3, K–Q5 or 7 ... R–Q5 leaves White helpless.

7	K–Q2	P–R5!
8	R–B7	P × P
9	R × P	R × P
10	R × P	K–K4
11	K–K2	R–B5
12	R–Kt6	R–QR5
13	R–Kt3	P–B5
14	R–Kt3	R–B5
15	K–Q1	K–K5

Preparing to force through the Bishop's Pawn. The King will

escort this passed Pawn to the queening-square.

16	P–KR4	P–B6
17	K–KI	K–B5
18	P–R5	R–B8*ch!*

One of the things that distinguishes the master from the amateur is that the former always tries to *simplify* even the easiest tasks. Thus, instead of unthinkingly taking the seventh rank at once (which, of course, is also good enough), Black gains a clear move.

19	K–B2	R–B7*ch*
20	K–KI	K–Kt6
21	P–R6	R–K7*ch!*

Another fine gain of time. It now 22 K–B1, R–KR7 threatening mate. Thus White's King is driven off.

| 22 | K–QI | R–KR7 |
| 23 | P–R4 | P–Kt5 |

... P × P also wins.

24	P–R7	R × P
25	R × P	R–R8*ch*
26	K–Q2	P–B7

And White resigned a few moves later. A crystal-clear ending by Tchigorin.

EXAMPLE 7

White to move

(Pasadena, 1932)

FACTOR

REINFELD

White's positional advantage is enormous. His King will take up a powerful position in the center, ready to shift to either wing. His Rook has the choice of invading Black's position either *via* the Queen or King Bishop file. His Pawns are in no danger, while Black's Pawns are weak, especially the Queen's Bishop Pawn and the King's Rook Pawn. Black's King is limited to defensive play; and the same is true of his Rook, which has an embarrassing lack of scope.

1 R–Q2ch   K–K2

The plausible 1 ... K–K3? would lose a whole Rook by *Zugzwang!*—2 K–Q4, P–R4; 3 R–KB2!, P–Kt5; 4 P × P, P × P; 5 R–B3, P–Kt6; 6 R × P, K–B3; 7 R–B3ch, K–K3; 8 R–B2 (or 8 R–B1) and the Rook is lost! A drastic example of Black's lack of mobility.

2 K–Q4   R–K3
3 P–K5

One move of the passed Pawn suffices to stalemate the Rook! The text prevents ... R–B3 and makes room for K–K4–B5. Black therefore prepares for his only chance: utilizing his Queen-side majority.

3 ....   P–R4
4 K–K4   K–K1
5 K–B5   R–K2
6 R–Q6

Decisive: if now 6 ... R–QKt2 (intending ... P–Kt5); 7 R × RP winning easily.

6 ....   R–B2ch

Seeking counterplay.

7 K–Kt6   R–B5
8 R × P   R × P

At this point White, being a young and inexperienced player, began to have some qualms about Black's dangerous-looking King's Knight Pawn; but a half-hour's reflection yielded the following forceful and pretty win. The remainder proceeds just as calculated, being based on the strength of the passed King's Rook Pawn which White soon obtains.

9 R–Kt6   P–Kt5
10 P × P   P × P

The alternative was 10 ... R × P; 11 K × P!, P–Kt5 (if 11 ... R × Rch; 12 P × R, K–Q1; 13 P–K6 and wins); 12 K–Kt7!, R × R (if 12 ... P–Kt6; 13 R–Kt6 followed by the advance of the Rook's Pawn); 13 P × R,

K–Q1; 14 P–K6, P–Kt6; 15
P–Kt7, K–B2; 16 P–Kt8(Q)ch,
K × Q; 17 P–K7 and wins!

11 K × P	R–K5
12 K–Kt6!	P–Kt5

Or 12 ... R × P; 13 P–R6
and the Rook's Pawn marches in.

13 P–R6	P–KKt6
14 P–R7	R–R5

If 14 ... R–Kt5ch?; 15
K–R5 wins at once.

15 R × P!	P–Kt7
16 R–Kt1	R–R8

And now comes the point of
White's 9th move:

17 R–Kt1!!	R × R
18 P–R8(Q)ch	K–Q2
19 Q–R2	*Resigns*

EXAMPLE 8
White to move
(St. Petersburg, 1914)

The essentials of the position
are as follows: (1) White's King
is better placed: potential centralization at Q4 will stop Black's
passed Pawn, and leave White
with easy access to either wing;
(2) White will have a *distant
passed Pawn* after the intended
P–B5.

RUBINSTEIN

DR. LASKER

Now see to what use the great
Lasker puts these advantages:

　1 P–B5!

Threatens 2 P × P!, R × R; 3
P–Kt7 and the Pawn queens.

　1 ....　　　　P × P

Or 1 ... P–Kt4; 2 P–B6,
K–Q3; 3 K–Q4, K–K3; 4
P–Kt4! and Black is helpless (if
4 ... R × P; 5 R × Rch, K × R;
6 K × P and White captures the
Queen's Knight Pawn with an
easy win). This variation gives
us the motif for the following
play: Black is always forced by
Zugzwang into a lost King and
Pawn ending.

　2 P × P　　　　R–B3

The sooner the passed Pawn is
stopped, the better.

3 R–B4!

The *Zugzwang* motif is now obvious. Black must either withdraw his King, advance a Pawn, or retreat his Rook—all disadvantageous possibilities.

3 ....   P–Kt5

3 ... K–Q3; 4 K–Q4, P–Kt5; 5 P–Kt3 transposes into the text. Or if 3 ... P–Q5; 4 K–K4, K–Q3 (on 4 ... K–B5; 5 K–K5 wins); 5 K×P and White must win.

4 P–Kt3!   R–B2

Allowing the passed Pawn to advance; but 4 ... K–Q3; 5 K–Q4 is no better.

5	P–B6	K–Q3
6	K–Q4!	K–K3
7	R–B2!	K–Q3

Again Black has no choice: if 7 ... R×P; 8 R×R*ch*, K×R;

9 K×P, K–K2; 10 K–B5 and wins.

8 R–QR2!

The horizontal Rook maneuver! If now 8 ... R×P; 9 R–R6*ch* again forces a won King and Pawn ending. Black must continue to give way.

8	....	R–B2
9	R–R6*ch*	K–Q2
10	R–Kt6	*Resigns*

For he has been deprived of any possible counterchance with ... R–B6. A splendid example of the value of *Zugzwang* and the utilization of simplifying threats.

EXAMPLE 9

White to move

(Carlsbad, 1907)

COHN

RUBINSTEIN

Spielmann appraises the position as follows: "White has several microscopic advantages. His King is placed more effectively, his Rook has an open file; whereas Black's Rook has little scope. Above all, White has the better Pawn position, for his Pawns are divided into two groups, his opponent's into three. And the saying 'in unity there is strength' is especially true of chess play. Connected Pawns protect each other automatically, and as a rule only one of them has to be protected by a piece. Scattered Pawns, on the other hand, often make too many demands on protective forces and easily succumb to hostile attack. In the present case, the isolated King's Pawn is the primary source of all of Black's difficulties."

1	K–K4	K–K3
2	R–R3!	P–R3
3	R–Kt3	K–B3

Allowing White's King to penetrate with decisive effect. However, if 3 ... P–Kt4; 4 P–R4! (threatening 5 P×P, P×P; 6 R×P!, R×P; 7 R×P*ch* followed by 8 R–Q5*ch* or 8 R–B5*ch*, depending how Black's King moves, followed by 9 R–Q3 or 9 R–B3 etc.), P×P; 5 R–Kt6*ch*, K–Q2; 6 R×R, K×R; 7 K×P and wins.

4	K–Q5!	R–K3
5	R–B3*ch*	K–K2
6	P–Kt3!	P–Kt3

Else 7 R–B5.

7	R–K3!	K–B3

White has blockaded the passed Pawn and at the same time forced Black's King away from White's potential passed Pawn.

8 P–B4!

Creating a passed Pawn! It is supported by the White King, and cannot be menaced by the Black King.

8	....	P×P
9	P×P	R–K1
10	R–B3*ch!*	

Driving Black's King still further away!

10	....	K–Kt4
11	P–B5	P–K5

Or 11 ... K–Kt5; 12 R–K3,
K–B4; 13 P–B6, R–Q1ch; 14
K–B5, K–K3; 15 P–B7 followed
by K–B6–Kt7 winning.

12	P–R4ch!	K–Kt5
13	R–B4ch	K×P
14	R×P	R–QR1
15	P–B6	P–Kt4
16	P×P	P×P
17	P–B7	K–B6
18	R–K1	Resigns

If 18 ... P–Kt5; 19 K–B6,
P–Kt6; 20 K–Kt7, R–KKt1;
21 P–B8(Q), R×Q; 22 K×R,
P–Kt7; 23 K–Kt7, K–B7; 24
R–QR1, P–Kt8(Q); 25 R×Q,
K×R; 26 K×P and wins. A
masterpiece by the wizard of this
type of ending.

EXAMPLE 10

White to move

(Nottingham, 1936)

Black is afflicted with two
glaring weaknesses: his Queen's
Rook Pawn and Queen's Bishop
Pawn. They must (and can) be
kept under constant pressure.
White's Rook is *aggressive*, Black's
Rook *passive*. The relation between the Kings is the same; for
since White's Pawn position is
perfectly secure, it requires no

VIDMAR

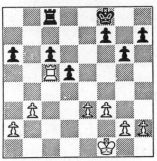

FLOHR

protection from the King, who
therefore heads for Q4.

1	K–K2	K–K2
2	K–Q3	K–Q3
3	R–R5!	R–QR1
4	K–Q4	P–B4
5	P–QKt4!	

The weak Black Pawns are
fixed, and White's King is estab-
lished at a dominating post.

5	....	R–QKt1
6	P–QR3	R–QR1
7	P–K4!	

An important step forward.
By opening up the whole length
of the fifth rank, White greatly
increases his Rook's mobility.

7	....	BP×P
8	P×P	P×P
9	K×P	R–R2

10 K–B4!   P–R3

Creating a new weakness; but he had to prevent K–Kt5–B6.

11 P–KR4   K–K3
12 K–Kt4   R–R1

Back and forth—such is his sad fate.

13 P–R5!   P–Kt4

A new weakness has been forced in Black's position.

14 P–Kt3   R–R2
15 K–B3   R–R1
16 K–K4   R–R2
17 K–Q4   K–Q3
18 K–K4   K–K3
19 R–K5ch!

Forcing Black's King to desert one side or the other. Which wing should he choose?!

19 ....   K–Q3

Or 19 ... K–B3; 20 R–B5, R–QB2; 21 P–R4, K–K3; 22 P–Kt5, K–Q3; 23 R×Pch, R×R; 24 P×R, K×P; 25 K–B5 and wins.

20 R–K8   P–B4

If 20 ... R–K2ch; 21 R×R, K×R; 22 K–K5 and wins: 22 ... K–B2 allows 23 K–Q6, while 22 ... K–Q2 allows 23 K–B6.

21 R–Q8ch!

Crushing. If 21 ... K–K2 or 21 ... K–B2; 22 R–KR8 wins the King's Rook Pawn because of the threatened 23 R–R7ch.

21 ....   K–B3
22 R–B8ch   K–Kt3

No better is 22 ... K–Kt4; 23 R×Pch, K–R5; 24 R–R5ch, K–Kt6; 25 K–B5 etc.

23 R×P   R–R2
24 R–K5   K–B3
25 R–K6ch   K–Kt4
26 K–B5   R–B2ch
27 R–B6   *Resigns*

For he must lose both King-side Pawns. Flawless play by a master technician! Horizontal Rook maneuvering played a vital role.

Bishop vs. *Knight Endings*

For many years there has been a good deal of heated controversy as to the relative merits of the Bishop and Knight. Opinion has varied. In the first half of the nineteenth century, the Knight was generally considered the stronger piece. Steinitz favored the Bishop, but it took several decades of propagandizing to spread this view.

Nowadays, most manuals tell us that one cannot assert dogmatically that the Bishop or Knight is the stronger piece; it all depends on the specific position. This is all very well, but now the question arises: just how does any given position affect the strength of these pieces relative to each other?

WHEN THE BISHOP IS SUPERIOR. First, let us consider the simplest possibility: when the player who has the Bishop against the Knight also has an advantage in material. What *systematic methods* may be applied to many, if not all, positions of this type?

In positions where you are a Pawn ahead, you should strive to convert your Pawn preponderance (located in that part of the board where your extra Pawn is placed) into a *passed Pawn.* This Pawn should then be advanced as far as is consonant with its safety. The opponent will have to use his King or Knight to prevent the further advance of this Pawn. You will then have an opportunity to break through on some other part of the board and attack unguarded units. This general process will be observed repeatedly in the endings that follow.

The Knight often cuts a sorry figure as a defender: if he is used to hold back the passed Pawn, his mobility is greatly diminished and he will often be unable to reach a threatened square (say on the other side of the board) in time.

Furthermore, we know that as the Knight reaches any one of the four sides of the board, his mobility is greatly decreased. This condition arises automatically when the Knight has to blockade a far-advanced passed Pawn which has reached the sixth or seventh rank. See Example 12 (p. 106) for an instance of the Knight's helplessness.

The final point which crops up so often in this winning process is that the weaker side, sooner or later, has to keep the Knight on a certain square to prevent the winning advance of the hostile passed Pawn, and also has to keep his King on a specific square to prevent the penetration of the stronger side's King. The result is very often *Zugzwang*; King or Knight must give way, with catastrophic consequences.

Where the forces are even, it is important to consider any positional advantages that may be present. These take the four following forms:

(1) The Pawns are even, but they are distributed in such a way that the player with the Bishop has a *distant passed Pawn*. (*Example:* with both Kings on the King-side, White, the player with the Bishop, has two Pawns on the King-side and one on the Queen-side; Black, who has the Knight, has three Pawns on the King-side.) In such cases the player with the Bishop has the advantage, because by advancing the free Pawn he may be able to tie up his opponent's pieces, *and then break through on the wing where his adversary has the Pawn majority.*

(2) A more complicated application of the above appears where the material is equal, but the Pawns unevenly distributed, one side having a Pawn majority on one wing, and the other player having a corresponding majority on the other wing. Such positions almost always favor the Bishop's side.

The latter advances his Pawns on the wing where he has a majority, and creates a passed Pawn, leading to the situation just described. If the other player imitates the process, it must be borne in mind that the Bishop can command several parts of the board at the same time, making it possible to aid his own passed Pawn and hold back the enemy's.

(3) It is important, when you have a Bishop, to keep your Pawns on the other color. (*Example:* your Bishop moves on

white squares. Place your Pawns on black squares.) Try to force your opponent to put his Pawns on the same color as that of your Bishop, which will then have plenty of targets to attack. At the same time, your King will be threatening to invade all those squares of the color opposite to that on which the Pawns are placed.

(4) Of course, you must always be on the lookout for weaknesses in Pawn structure (isolated Pawns, backward Pawns, weak color complexes etc.). Be alert to seize such positional advantages as strong centralization; creation of new diagonals for your Bishop; Pawn majorities; passed Pawns; and the like.

EXAMPLES FROM ACTUAL PLAY

EXAMPLE 11

White to move

(Barmen, 1905)

TCHIGORIN

BERGER

Despite the greatly reduced material, White has a forced win!

The Knight, placed unfavorably *at the edge of the board*, is here seen at his worst.

1 B–K5!

The Knight is now stalemated, and in effect we have a King and Pawn ending which is very easily won for White.

1	....	K–K1
2	K×P	K–K2
3	K–Kt7	K–K3
4	P–B6!	K×B
5	P–B7	*Resigns*

The Knight has acquitted himself very badly! On the other hand, the splendidly centralized Bishop has shown to great advantage.

EXAMPLE 12

White to move

(Carlsbad, 1907)

JANOWSKI

NIMZOVICH

White is a Pawn ahead, and a distant passed Pawn at that. For a player of master strength, the winning process is a simple technical problem. The distant passed Pawn will keep Black's King busy on the Queen-side, whereupon White's King will break through on the King-side. The fact that two of Black's Pawns have been *moved* is a great help to White.

First, White's King *heads for the center*—a maneuver which must be imitated by Black; for White's King must not be allowed to reach Q5 (or QB5, if the Knight moves).

1 K–B3   K–K2

2 K–K3   P–B3

An unfortunate necessity, if his King is to reach Q3. But now his Knight's Pawn has been weakened.

3 K–Q4   K–Q3
4 B–Q1   Kt–Kt3
5 B–B3   Kt–B1
6 P–R4!   Kt–K2
7 B–K4!

White's Bishop takes the right diagonal: the attack on the Knight's Pawn leads to a fatal weakness in Black's camp.

7 ....   P–Kt4

This loses in an instructive manner; but Black cannot move his Knight, and King moves allow White's King to reach QB5 with decisive effect. The only alternative is a Pawn move:

I. 7 ... P–B4; 8 B–B3, Kt–B1; 9 B–Q5, Kt–K2; 10

B–B7, K–Q2; 11 K–K5 and wins.

II. 7 ... P–R4; 8 P–Kt3!, P–B4; 9 B–B3, Kt–B1; 10 B–Q5, Kt–K2; 11 B–B7, K–Q2; 12 K–K5 etc.

8 BP×P	BP×P
9 P×P	P×P
10 P–Kt6	P–Kt5
11 P–Kt7	

Note throughout how the distant passed Pawn paralyzes Black's King.

11	K–B2
12 K–K5	P–Kt6
13 K–B4	Kt–Kt1
14 K×P	Kt–B3
15 B–B3	Kt–Q2

Guarding the queening-square so that Black's King can cross to the other side. But it is much too late.

16 K–B4	K–Q3
17 K–B5	K–K2
18 B–B6!	Kt–Kt1
19 B–Kt5	*Resigns*

Black's King can reach KKt2, blocking the further progress of White's King's Knight Pawn; but then the White King crosses to QB7 and wins the ice-bound Knight. A painful defeat for Janowski, who was himself so fond of the Bishops!

EXAMPLE 13

Black to move

(Gothenburg, 1920)

RUBINSTEIN

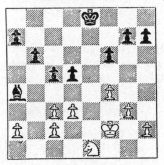

RETI

Black has a decided advantage here, as his Bishop is far more mobile than the Knight. At the moment the Knight is tied to the defense of the weak Pawn at QB2, but even if this piece could move, it could not land on the squares Q4, K4, K5 and KKt5. White's Queen-side Pawns are weak, and we shall soon see that he is vulnerable on the other wing as well.

1	K–K2
2 K–K3	K–K3
3 P–Kt4	

To keep Black's King out of KB4. Black now proceeds to exploit this weakness, which could not be avoided in the long run.

3	K–Q3
4 P–KR3	P–Kt3
5 K–Q2	B–Q2!
6 Kt–B3	K–K2!

Preventing P–Kt5. He wants this Pawn to remain on a white square, where it will be susceptible to attack by the far-ranging Bishop.

| 7 K–K3 | P–KR4! |

Reducing the Knight to a passive position, for if 8 P × P, P × P; 9 P–KR4, K–K3 followed by ... K–B4 etc.

| 8 Kt–R2 | K–Q3 |
| 9 K–K2 | |

9 P–Q4 would have held out longer. The text allows Black to win artistically.

| 9 .... | P–Q5! |

Decisively diminishing the King's mobility and at the same time giving his Bishop more scope.

| 10 BP × P | |

If 10 P–B4, P × P; 11 P × P (if 11 Kt × P, K–K3; 12 Kt–R6, P–KKt4! making ... K–K4 possible, so that White cannot simultaneously defend himself against the attack on his Pawns at

QB2 and KB4), P–KKt4! with a winning game.

10	BP × P
11 K–Q2	P × P
12 P × P	B–B3!

Keeping the Knight in his place.

13 K–K2

If 13 P–B3, P × P*ch*; 14 K × P, B–Kt7! (stalemating the Knight and threatening to establish *Zugzwang* with ... K–Q4); 15 K–Q4, P–QKt4; 16 K–K3, P–R4; 17 P–R3, K–Q4; 18 K–K2 (White must be on his guard against the coming distant passed Pawn; thus if 18 K–B2, P–Kt5!; 19 P × P, P–R5! wins), K–Q5; 19 K–Q2, P–R5 (with a standing threat of ... P–Kt5 at the appropriate moment); 20 P–Kt5, P–B4 and White must resign.

14 ....   B–Q4!

Forcing a distant passed Pawn.

15 P–R3   P–QKt4
16 Kt–Bl   P–R4
17 Kt–Q2   P–R5!

Now White must succumb to the double menace of ... P–Kt5 and ... P–Kt4.

18 Kt–K4*ch*   B×Kt
19 P×B   P–Kt5!
20 K–Q2   P×P

The distant passed Pawn!

21 K–Bl   P–Kt4!
    Resigns

For if 22 P×P (or 22 P–K5*ch*, P×P; 23 P×P, P–K5 etc.), P×P; 23 K–Kt1, K–K4; 24 K–R2, K×P; 25 K×P, K–B6 etc.

A great ending!

EXAMPLE 14

Black to move

(Hague, 1928)

White's Knight is well centralized, but the two most important squares it might want to reach (KB5 or QKt5) are already covered by the Bishop. Furthermore, White's Queen's Knight Pawn may require protection;

KASHDAN

STOLTZ

and, fortunately for Black, his King leads the race to the center. In the ending that follows, the Bishop's strength in endings with Pawns on both sides of the board is convincingly demonstrated.

(*The following notes are by Kashdan.*)

1 ....   K–Bl
2 K–Bl   K–K2
3 K–K2   K–Q3
4 K–Q3   K–Q4
5 P–R4

In order to place the Pawns on black squares, where the Bishop cannot attack them. But Black's King gains more chances to enter later. The further advanced position of the Black King is an important asset.

5 ....   B–Bl!

The check at R3 will force White's King to one side or the other, whereupon Black can advance on whichever side is left unguarded.

6 Kt–B3   B–R3*ch*
7 K–B3

If 7 K–K3, K–B4; 8 Kt–Kt5, K–Kt5; 9 Kt × BP, K × P and Black will soon win the Knight for the passed Pawn. Or 8 K–Q2, K–Kt5; 9 K–B2, B–Kt2*!*; 10 Kt–K1, B–Q4; 11 Kt–Q3*ch*, K–R6 winning a Pawn.

7 ....   P–R3

To keep the Knight out, preparatory to advancing the King.

8 Kt–Q4

If 8 Kt–Q2, B–K7 and White cannot maintain his defensive position.

8 ....   P–Kt3
9 Kt–B2   K–K5
10 Kt–K3   P–B4

The Knight is given no opportunity to take an effective post, and the White Pawns will gradually be weakened.

[See diagram, next column.]

11 K–Q2   P–B5
12 Kt–Kt4   P–R4
13 Kt–B6*ch*   K–B4
14 Kt–Q7

There is no good square. If 14 Kt–Q5, B–Kt2; 15 Kt–K7*ch?*, K–B3; 16 Kt–Kt8*ch*, K–B2; 17 Kt–R6*ch*, K–Kt2 and wins. The Knight must exercise care to avoid similar difficulties.

14 ....   B–B1

Not 14 ... K–Kt5; 15 Kt–K5*ch*. The text forces the win of a Pawn.

15 Kt–B8

If 15 Kt–B5, K–Kt5; 16 Kt–Q3, B–B4 wins the Rook's Pawn. Or 15 Kt–Kt8, B–Kt2; 16 P–B3, K–K3*!* followed by ... K–Q3–B2 winning.

15 ....   P–Kt4
16 P–Kt3

Forced, for if 16 P × P, K × P threatening ... K–R3–Kt2 and again the Knight is helpless.

16 ....   P × RP

17	P×RP	K–Kt5	24 K–Q5	P–B6!
18	Kt–Kt6	B–B4	25 P–Kt5	P–R6
19	Kt–K7	B–K3	26 Kt×P	P–R7
20	P–Kt4	K×P	27 P–Kt6	P–R8(Q)
21	K–Q3	K–Kt5		
22	K–K4	P–R5		*Resigns*
23	Kt–B6	B–B4*ch*		

If 23 ... P–R6; 24 Kt–K5*ch*, and 25 Kt–B3 will stop the Pawn. Black's next move ends this slim hope.

(This beautiful ending, played with such exactness and simplicity by Kashdan, seems to me to attain an unsurpassable level of chess artistry.)

WHEN THE KNIGHT IS SUPERIOR. So strong a case has been made for the Bishop that it might well seem that there was nothing to be said for the Knight. And yet this is not so. For, since the superiority of the Bishop, when it does exist, is based on certain positional factors, it follows that (1) the superiority of the Bishop evaporates once these factors are removed: (2) it is possible that there are other factors whose presence actually makes it a disadvantage to have a Bishop.

The chief instance in which it is a disadvantage to have a Bishop is a position where a player has difficulties with a *weak color complex.* This subject has already been treated several times (see particularly page 40), but it is worth explaining again in terms of its endgame application.

If you have all your Pawns on the same color, it follows that the squares of the other color are not commanded by your Pawns. (*Example:* White Pawns on QR3, QKt2, QB3, K3, KB2, KKt3, KR2. All the White Pawns are on black squares. His Pawns therefore have no control over the white squares.) Now, if you have a Bishop which is on the same-colored squares as your Pawns (in our example, on black squares), his deficiency in commanding the black squares is in no way alleviated.

Worse yet: there is the additional disadvantage that the Bishop, being on the same-colored squares as the Pawns, is seriously hampered in its movements by these Pawns.

Still another corollary: the squares of the opposite color (in our example, the white squares), being commanded neither by the Bishop nor by the Pawns, are completely at the mercy of the hostile pieces, which have the opportunity to get a foothold on the unprotected squares.

It will be found that in actual play with forces even, weak color complexes give the Knight the upper hand.

EXAMPLES FROM ACTUAL PLAY

EXAMPLE 15

Black to move

(Bled, 1931)

NIMZOVICH

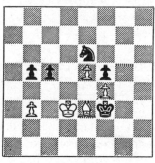

COLLE

The material is greatly reduced; yet the limited mobility of the Bishop (*hemmed in by the Pawns on black squares*) is the point of departure for a beautiful winning

process. This procedure is far from easy, as Black must keep an eye on White's passed King's Pawn. Black begins with several judicious gains of tempi:

1 ....   P–B5*ch*

Of course not 1 ... Kt × P*ch??*; 2 B × Kt, K × B; 3 P–K6 and White wins.

2 P × P   P × P*ch*
3 K–Q2

Hoping for 3 ... P–B6*ch?*; 4 K–Q3, P–B7; 5 B–B1, Kt × P *ch*; 6 K × P and the draw is certain.

3 ....   K–K5*!*

Posting his King more effectively and forcing the following move, which gives Black a decisive tempo for advancing his passed Pawn.

4 K–K2	P–B6
5 B–B1	

Again forced. But now Black gains the vital square Q6 for his King.

5	Kt–Q5*ch*
6 K–Q1	K–Q6
7 B–R3	

Another forced move; but it seems that Black can make no further progress, as his Knight must keep an eye on the King's Pawn (7 ... P–B7*ch*; 8 K–K1*!*, Kt–K7*??*; 9 P–K6).

7	Kt–Kt4*!?*

So that if 8 P–K6, P–B7*ch!* (not 8 ... Kt × B*?*); 9 K–B1, Kt–Q5*!* and the double threat of ... Kt–Kt6*ch* or ... Kt–K7*ch* wins at once.

However, 7 ... Kt–B6*!!* would have won even more rapidly.

8 B–B1

If 8 B–B5, P–B7*ch*; 9 K–B1, Kt–B6*!* wins.

8	Kt–Q5*!*

If now 9 K–K1, K–B7; 10 B–K3, Kt–K3 followed by 11 ... K–Kt8 winning the Bishop for the Queen's Bishop Pawn.

9 B–R3	Kt–B6*!!*

This decides very quickly (see the note to Black's seventh move).

10 B–B5

If 10 B–B1, P–B7 *mate!*. Or 10 P–K6, P–B7*ch*; 11 K–B1, Kt–Q5 and wins!

10	P–B7*ch*
11 K–B1	Kt–Q7
	Resigns

For if 12 K–Kt2, Kt–Kt6 etc. Or 12 B–K3, K × B; 13 K × P, Kt–K5 stopping the King's Pawn.

An exquisite study, composed in actual play! The agile hopping moves of the Knight have rarely been used to such advantage. Nimzovich was a wizard!

EXAMPLE 16

White to move

(Monte Carlo, 1902)

PILLSBURY

MARCO

Black's position is riddled with weaknesses: the doubled, isolated Queen's Bishop Pawn and the artificially isolated Knight's Pawn, which is already doomed. Added to these *organic* weaknesses is Black's pitiable lack of mobility. The win simply goes on wheels:

1 P–R3*!*

Taking away Black's only counterchance (... K–Kt5).

1 ....   K–Kt3

2 K–Q4

It is important to prevent ... K–B4.

2 ....   P–B4*ch*

Creating a new weakness; but if the Bishop goes back and forth, White wins easily with Kt–Q1–B3–K4.

3 K–Q3	K–B3
4 Kt–Q1	B–Q2
5 Kt–B3	K–Kt2
6 Kt–K4	K–B1

Black could just as well resign, and spare himself the mournful proceedings which follow.

7 Kt × KtP	B–K1
8 Kt–K4	B–B3
9 P–B4	K–Q2
10 Kt × P*ch*	K–K2
11 Kt–K4	B–R1
12 K–Q4	B–Kt2
13 P–KB5	B–B3

He is helpless against the oncoming Pawns.

14 P–Kt5	B–R1
15 Kt–B5	B–B3

16	P–B6ch	K–K1
17	P–K6	P×P
18	P–Kt6	B–B6
19	Kt×P	Resigns

EXAMPLE 17
White to move

(Match: Great Britain
—Holland, 1937)

LANDAU

THOMAS

Black has played the previous phase of this ending very badly, as may be seen from the fact that almost all his Pawns are on white squares, so that: (1) his Bishop has hardly any mobility, and is limited to strictly defensive functions; (2) the black squares are all under White's control, giving him ideal posts for his King at K5 and his Knight at Q4; (3)

Black's Queen's Pawn is blockaded and therefore worthless, whereas White's Queen-side majority of Pawns is really effective.

1	Kt–Kt4	B–Q2
2	Kt–B2!	B–K1
3	P–QKt4	B–Q2
4	Kt–Q4	

The Knight is beautifully posted here: he attacks the weak Bishop's Pawn, prepares for P–Kt5, blocks the Queen's Pawn—and cannot be driven away!

| 4 | .... | B–K1 |
| 5 | P–QR4 | P–QR3 |

Now all the Black Pawns are on white squares and White's King is ready for an invasion of the black squares.

| 6 | P–R5! | B–Q2 |
| 7 | P–Kt5! | BP×P |

If 7 ... RP×P; 8 P–R6, B–B1; 9 Kt×Pch, K–Q2; 10 Kt–Kt4 winning easily. Black's Bishop is smothered.

| 8 | K×P | B–K1 |
| 9 | Kt–B2! | |

Now the weak point, Black's Queen's Rook Pawn, must be kept under observation.

| 9 | .... | B–Q2 |
| 10 | Kt–Kt4 | B–B1 |

The Knight is still attacking, the Bishop still defending.

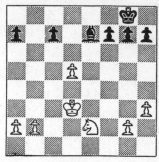

TCHIGORIN

| 11 K–B6 | K–Q1 |
| 12 K–Q6 | |

White maneuvers very cleverly. 12 ... K–K1 can now be answered by 13 K–B7 with an easy win.

12	B–Kt2
13 P–B6	B–B1
14 P–B7*ch*	K–K1
15 K–B6	K–B2

If instead 15 ... P–Kt4; 16 K–Kt6, K–Q2; 17 Kt×P, B×Kt; 18 K×B, P–Kt5 (or 18 ... K×P; 19 K×P etc.); 19 K–Kt7 etc.

16 K–Kt6	K–K3
17 Kt×P	K–Q3
18 Kt–Kt4	*Resigns*

EXAMPLE 18
White to move
(Budapest, 1896)

Black's great weakness is his Queen-side, the isolated Pawns being welcome targets. In addition, they are on black squares, which means that (1) it is easy to obtain access to the Pawns, as all the white squares in the vicinity are weak; (2) the Bishop's mobility will be greatly restricted by the need for protecting the weak Pawns. Under the circumstances, Black's King-side majority of Pawns is of little value.

1 K–B4	K–B1
2 K–Kt5	K–K1
3 K–R6	B–B4
4 K–Kt5	B–K6

He centralizes the Bishop, so as to have it available for action on either wing.

| 5 K–B6 | K–Q1 |
| 6 P–QKt4 | P–KR4 |

7 P–QR4   B–Q7
8 P–Kt5   P–R5?

Fixing both White Pawns on the King-side, but every placement of a Pawn on black squares means less mobility and more defensive work for the Bishop. ... P–Kt3 was preferable.

9 Kt–Q4

Threatening to win a Pawn by 10 Kt–B3.

Black's game has now become very difficult: if 9 ... B–Kt4; 10 Kt–B3, B–K2 (if 10 ... B–B3; 11 K–Kt7); 11 Kt–K5 (or 11 K–Kt7), P–B3; 12 Kt–Kt6 winning a Pawn.

Or 9 ... B–K8; 10 Kt–B5, P–Kt3; 11 Kt–R6, P–B3 (if 11 ... P–B4; 12 Kt–B7*ch*, K–K2; 13 Kt–K5, K–B3; 14 Kt–B3, B–Kt6; 21 K–Kt7—or 13 ... P–Kt4; 14 Kt–B3) 12 Kt–B7*ch*, K–B1; 13 Kt–R8, P–Kt4; 14 Kt–B7, B–Q7; 15 Kt–R6 and the Knight reaches B5 with much the same position as in the text. Instructive play!

9 ....   P–Kt4
10 Kt–B5   B–K8

Black's Pawn majority is paralyzed, and he cannot drive the Knight away from its powerful post.

11 Kt–R6

Another, even more forcing line is 11 P–Q6, P × P (or 11 ... B–R4; 12 P–Q7, B–Kt3; 13 Kt–R6, K–K2; 14 Kt × P and wins); 12 Kt × P, P–B3 (if 12 ... K–K2; 13 Kt–B8*ch*); 13 Kt–K4 (the power of the Knight is enormous), K–K2; 14 K–Kt7 and wins.

11 ....   P–B3
12 Kt–B5   B–Kt5
13 Kt–Q4   K–B1
14 Kt–K6   B–Q3

Or 14 ... B–R4; 15 Kt–B5 (threatening to win with Kt–K4. If 15 ... K–Q1?; 16 Kt–Kt7*ch*. The Knight is everywhere!), B–B6; 16 Kt–K4, B–K4; 17 P–Q6, P × P; 18 Kt × P*ch*, K–Kt1 (18 ... B × Kt leads to a lost King and Pawn ending, as all the King-side Pawns fall); 19 P–R5, K–R1; 20 P–Kt6, K–

Kt1; 21 Kt–K4!, K–R1; 22
Kt–B5 and wins.

15	P–R5	B–Kt5
16	P–Kt6!	RP×P
17	P×P	P×P
18	P–Q6	B×P

19	K×B	P–Kt4
20	Kt–Q4	P–QKt5
21	K–K6	*Resigns*

A most instructive ending, in which the Knight displays his customary agility.

Index